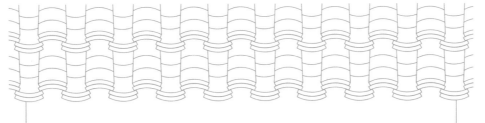

HISTORIC
HOUSES
IN FUJIAN

///////////////////////

• HISTORIC BLOCKHOUSES

QU LIMING / XIAO CHUNLEI

福建经典古民居

摄影＼曲利明

撰文＼萧春雷

古厝

海峡出版发行集团

海峡书局

图书在版编目（CIP）数据

福建经典古民居 / 曲利明等著. —— 福州 ：海峡书
局，2018.9
ISBN 978-7-5567-0512-2

Ⅰ. ①福… Ⅱ. ①曲… Ⅲ. ①民居－古建筑－研究－
福建 Ⅳ. ①K928.71

中国版本图书馆CIP数据核字（2018）第135496号

主编、摄影：曲利明

撰　　　文：何葆国　萧春雷　陈文波

责 任 编 辑：廖飞琴　林前汐　陈婧　卢佳颖　胡悦　陈洁蕾　俞晓佳

装 帧 设 计：黄舒堉　李晔　董玲芝

英 文 翻 译：郭琳琳　（美）凯伦·杰南特　陈励　葛凯伦　陈泽平

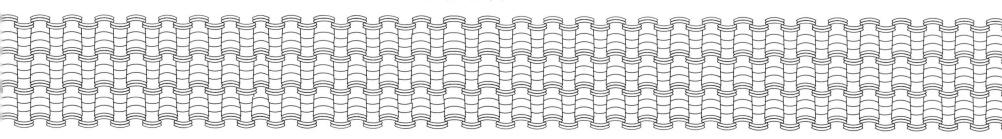

FÚJIÀNJĪNGDIĂNGŬMÍNJŪ

福建经典古民居

出版发行：海峡书局

地　　　址：福州市鼓楼区五一路北段110号

邮　　　编：350001

印　　　刷：深圳市泰和精品印刷有限公司

开　　　本：889毫米×1194 毫米　　1/12

印　　　张：106.5

图　　　文：1278码

版　　　次：2018年9月第1版

印　　　次：2018年9月第1次印刷

书　　　号：ISBN 978-7-5567-0512-2

定　　　价：1300.00元（全套）

目 录 CONTENTS

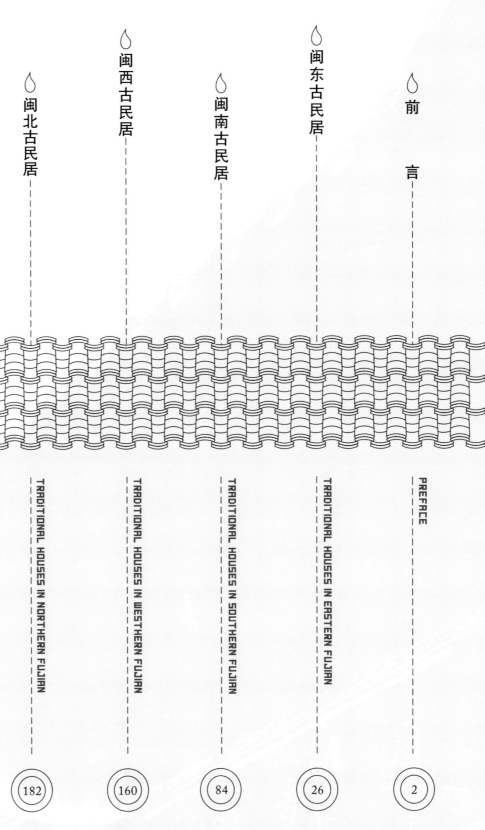

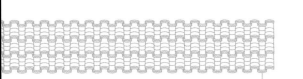

◎ 前　　　　　言 ◎

从闽西北一幢普通大厝说起

故乡就是家园。而家园，首先意味着一幢房屋。我的孩提时代是在闽西北一个河谷盆地里度过的。村庄紧依山脚一字排开，面向稻浪起伏的田野，一条小溪蜿蜒流过，对面矗立着险峻的红石山，以及重重叠叠的远山。我最初和最深刻的记忆，来自于村子里一幢烟熏火燎的老房子萧家大厝。

福建各地的许多村落，都能见到类似的场景。每个河谷盆地都藏着一个村庄，人们聚族而居，建造与萧家大厝差不多的房屋，让人感到十分亲切。

萧家大厝是典型的闽西北传统民居，背倚古木参天的后山，门前依次是空坪、水井、池塘、稻田。大厝五开间，前后两厅，左右风火墙外各有一排配房。从结构看，天井是大厝通风采光的中心，接受四面屋顶的落水，民间称四水归堂。而大厝的核心，显然是宽敞的正厅，那里有一个供奉萧氏始祖昭穆牌位的神龛，所有的重大仪式，例如祭祖与婚丧，都在这个厅堂举行。传统的中国民居，死者与生者混居，死者优先；一幢房屋最重要的位置必定是留给祖宗的。中国的建筑为什么讲究中轴线？因为只有这样，才能找出那个最重要的位置：居中；居上。

萧家是一个大家族，人丁兴旺，分家后的每个小家庭都分得正厅或前厅旁的房屋一两间，不够住，就在附近另建新房。上世纪末，萧家大厝只剩两三户人家留守，绝大多数都搬到新建的砖混结构的房子里去了。曾经深情庇护过一个家族两三百年的萧家大厝，被人遗弃，在短短20年间，进入风烛残年。因为数十户人家对这幢祖宅拥有产权，任何改变事实上都是不可能的，等待它的命运就是不断地衰败，腐朽，坍塌。

这也是绝大多数传统民居在今天的命运。我们的生活方式发生了巨大变化，传统建筑难以满足我们对住宅的多方面需求，正在迅速退出历史舞台，被拆毁，或者被遗弃。几千年来中华民族累积下来的悠久的建筑文明，除了个别作为文物加以保护，大多数将在半个世纪内消失。历史像被一把快刀斩过。

福建的地理与文化板块

要理解福建民居，首先要了解福建的地理、语言、人民。建筑传统是文化传统的一部分，先于我们而存在，又因我们而改变。闽南人去了台湾或南洋，建造的还是红砖大厝；欧洲人在厦门鼓浪屿建房子，范本是万里之外的西洋别墅。然而，它们都根据当地的地理和气候条件有所变化，新添一些元素，渐成风格。

从地理看，福建号称东南山国，东南临海，与台湾相望，东北、西北、西南三面分别有高大的山脉与浙江、江西、广东分界，自成一个地理单元。其中，山地和丘陵面积占80%以上，素有"八山一水一分田"之称。与海岸线平行

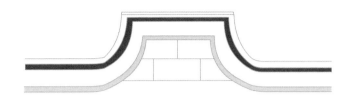

的两条绵延五百多公里的大山脉——斜贯西北边境的武夷山脉、斜贯闽中的戴云山脉把福建纵向切割成西北山区和东南沿海两部分。

福建的河流多半往东南方向入海，对西北方向的山地进行横向切割，从而形成散碎的区域。最大的河流闽江，其三大支流沙溪、富屯溪、建溪发源于西北武夷山脉，汇聚于南平，流经福州入海，贯通闽北山区和闽东沿海。发源于中部山系的闽东南几条主要河流，如木兰溪、晋江、九龙江，流程短，有较大的冲积平原，流域间相互联系比较紧密。闽西的汀江则由广东注入韩江，闽西与粤东同属客家区域。

福建简称"闽"。大体说来，福建可以分为四个地区：闽江上游（古代建宁、延平、邵武三府）的闽北地区；闽江下游及东北沿海（古代福州、福宁两府）的闽东地区；南部沿海（古代漳州、泉州、兴化三府）的闽南地区；西南山区（古代汀州府）客家人聚居的闽西地区。其中，个别县市因历史沿革而有所变迁，比如，兴化府的莆田、仙游，宋代就从泉州府独立出来，语言和文化有自己的特色，人们通常视为独立的区域，很少包括在闽南范围；而龙岩、漳平，本该属闽南地区，现今在行政区划上却划归闽西地区。

福建的语言非常复杂。李如龙《福建方言》把福建分为七个大方言区：闽东方言区，其代表是福州话；莆仙方言区；闽南方言区，现今的代表是厦门话；闽北方言区，其代表是建瓯话；闽中方言区，其代表是永安话；闽西客家方言区，其代表是长汀话；闽西北赣方言区，其代表是邵武话。我们如果把闽中方言和闽西北方言看成闽北方言的变体，就会简单得多，只剩闽北话、闽东话、闽南话、闽西话，再加一个莆仙话。福建各个方言区与地理区域的划分基本是重合的。

方言的差异通常还意味着人民与文化的差异。陈支平《福建六大民系》将福建人分为六个民系：闽北人，闽东（福州）人，闽南人，闽西（客家）人，兴化人，龙岩人。各个民系创造了不同的地方特色文化，例如闽北的理学文化，闽东的官宦文化，闽南的海洋文化，闽西的农耕文化，莆仙的科举文化，龙岩的商业文化。而种种文化差异，直接影响到各地的建筑形态，于是出现了多姿多彩的福建民居。

现在的行政区划，有的突破了地域的文化属性。1970年，闽中设三明地区，后改为三明市，从闽北和闽西各划出数县，组建成一个新的地区。于是人们开始说闽西北这个概念。闽西北从来不是一个文化概念，历史上泰宁县、建宁县隶属邵武府，将乐县和沙县隶属延平府，属于闽北文化系统；宁化县、清流县、明溪县隶属汀州府，属于闽西文化系统。谈到文化，我们不得不回到文化生成的历史年代。

自秦设闽中郡以来，福建一直是一个单独的行政板块，疆域变动不大。同时，因为处处崇山峻岭，内部交往困难，各个区域相对独立，有自己的发展脉络。汉唐之后，北方汉民大量移居福建，闽北、闽东和闽南地区先后得以开

发。两宋三百年，闽北文化大放光芒，以朱熹为代表的闽学将福建文化推上顶峰，标志着中古时代华夏民族的思想深度。闽东文化在一千年里表现得相当稳健，清中叶以后却有了一个大爆发，出现"晚清人物数侯官"的盛况。莆仙为文献名邦，由宋至明中期，一直领袖全闽，可惜1562年被倭寇攻破府城，逐渐消沉。泉州虽然是宋元时期的国际大港，人文荟萃，但一直到明清两代，闽南文化才异军突起，呈现海洋文明的华彩。闽西开发较迟，宋以后汉族移民才大量从赣南迁入，并形成独特的客家民系，其文化在明清之际开始引人注目。

福建的传统民居，也因闽文化的多元组合，变得丰富多彩。从闽北的青砖灰瓦，到闽南的红砖红瓦，再到闽西南的圆形土楼，反差是何等剧烈！全国各地很少像福建拥有这么丰富的民居类型。当然，每一种民居类型，都不是偶然形成的，它必定深深奠基于人民的生活方式之中。

闽北古民居：华美的雕花门楼

闽江上游三大支流的广大流域，历史上分属闽北三府十七县管辖。建溪流域诸县属建宁府，府治在今建瓯市；富屯溪流域上游诸县属邵武府；富屯溪下游和沙溪中下游流域诸县属延平府，府治在今南平市。闽北地区的特点是山高林深，河流湍急，平地很少，但由于与江西、浙江接壤，成为北方汉族移民入闽的第一站，开发最早。

汉晋时期开始入闽的移民，在闽北定居下来，男耕女织，秋收冬藏。宋代的闽北已进入文化高度成熟时期，科举繁盛，人才众多，还涌现了朱熹、李纲、杨时、真德秀、柳永、严羽等一批著名人物。所谓闽学，其骨干朱熹及其师友弟子多半是闽北人，并且主要在闽北发展，逐渐形成一个重要学派。无论思想深度还是影响力，闽学堪称福建文化的一个顶峰。

明中叶以后，由于战乱等原因，闽北文化开始衰弱，但是理学传统的深厚积淀，依然表现在各个方面。闽北的建筑，肃穆质朴，英华内敛，呈现出一种理性与节制之美。众多豪门大宅，混杂在寻常巷陌，只有登堂入室，细细品味，才能领略其深沉的意味。

泰宁的尚书第就是这样一个例子。所谓尚书第是明朝泰宁籍兵部尚书李春烨的府第，门面小而朴实，夹杂在一大片明清建筑群中。然而进入甬道，你会发现这是一座庞大的建筑，五幢三进院落一字排开，气势恢弘。传统的三厅九栋布局，幢与幢之间既独立，又有回廊与侧门沟通。简练的石雕，粗大的梁柱，深邃的庭院，都充分体现明代建筑的雄浑大气。现存福建古民居多建于清代，明代的十分罕见，论规模之大、保存之完好，尚书第为绝无仅有的一座。

尚书第大量使用了花岗岩。事实上，因为采石不易，闽北建筑里石材的使用十分俭省，只在门楼、天井、走廊、檐阶等少数地方铺设。比较气派的闽北建筑，多为砖木结构，寻常人家则使用土木材料。

从前闽北人建房子，并不复杂。先弄堆石料来做地基，没有方石，就去河

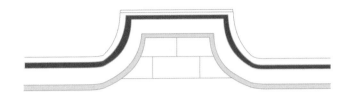

里找鹅卵石。瓦片当然是必需的。而最重要的是上山砍来一堆大杉木。杉木是闽北的特产，树干直，重量轻，木中所含杉脑可防虫蛀，是理想的建筑材料。一幢普通的房屋可以全由杉材建成，并且不施油漆，叫清水杉。逢年过节，用水刷洗板壁，便露出黄褐的杉木本色，仿佛宋元古画，花纹诱人。房屋的木构部分建成后，就可以入住了。如果你想结实点，农闲时请几个亲朋好友帮忙夯土墙，做个围护。如果你有经济实力，改砌砖墙，再搞个精美的雕花门楼，就足以炫耀乡里了。

典型的闽北建筑受徽派建筑影响较深，青砖灰瓦，朴素大方；普通人家的屋脊都是平直的，只在檐角起翘，像伊秉绶隶书里的刚劲而短促的燕尾；高大的马头墙错落起伏，形成梯级节奏。其质朴的造型，刚硬的风骨，深沉的色调，都让人想起仁义礼智忠孝节悌这些传统价值观。闽北建筑也有华丽的成分，那就是砖雕。朴拙厚实的青砖，一旦雕上栩栩如生的花草鸟兽、神仙人物、戏曲故事，就有了灵气，像黑白照片那样纯净雅致。在武夷山五夫里的连氏节孝坊，那面精彩绝伦的雕花门楼混杂在一片老旧建筑中，孤立无援，仿佛幽雅贞静的古典女子沦落街头。现在还保存着最多精美砖雕的，也许是武夷山市的下梅村，数十幢古民居的门楼，极尽雕饰之能事。那天傍晚，我看到斜阳照耀着邹氏家祠门楼洋洋洒洒铺排开来的雕花图案，锦缎一般绚烂。

闽北的木雕也是很精彩的。邵武金坑有座名叫儒林郎的建筑，六扇镂空的隔扇门，左右厢房窗格，到处雕刻春兰夏荷、苏武牧羊、喜鹊登梅等图案。刀法明快，构图简洁，意趣动人。这是我在普通民居中见到的最出色的木雕艺术。

闽北的古民居，都默默隐藏在乡村里，无声无息地老去。有一次，我们在建瓯寻找一个叫五石的小村子。荒野里，路很小，我们正疑惑这里不像有村庄。没想到小村子猛然显现，村里居然矗立着三幢装饰极其精美的老宅。清代工匠的细致和耐心让我们叹服。柱础、柱头、斗拱、梁枋、窗格、花板，一切可装饰的部分，无不精雕细刻，美轮美奂；两个藻井的修辞更是铺张扬厉，极尽奢华；壁画和彩绘依然生动传神。最奇妙的是，当初的浓墨重彩，经过百余年沉淀，已经归于淡雅。一种意味深长的宁静开始生长。

房子的主人不在，一条狗懒洋洋地趴在大厅一角。虽然只有两个儿童在走动、说话，但古宅里竟然回荡着金属般的声音。

我们离开时，村口的一位妇女说："都是破房子，有什么好看的？"

一幢老房子，不仅是人类的作品，也是时间的作品。或者说，人类和时间在创造中共谋。光人类是不能抵达事物的核心的，还要潮水般的光阴来冲刷。最后，伪饰剥落，事物显露内心，如同鹅卵石裸露最深邃的断裂。

闽东古民居：飞腾的风火墙

闽东地区包括两个部分，闽江下游的福州地区和古代福宁府（府治在今霞浦）管辖的闽东各县。两地虽然都属于闽东方言区，但地理、经济和文

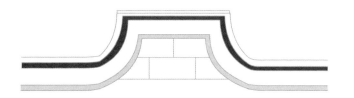

化等方面，都存在极大的差异。

福州坐落在闽江下游临近出海口的冲积盆地上，开阔平坦，土地肥沃，东有高山阻挡台风，却不妨海潮直抵城下。江海交汇，上控下引，福州的地理位置十分重要。宋代名臣蔡襄形容说："福建一路州军，建、剑、汀州、邵武军，连接两浙江南路，乘船下水三两日可至福州城下。其东界连接温州，并南接兴化军，泉州漳州各在海畔，四向舟船可至闽中。诸州皆以福州为根本。"福州先天具有成为福建政治中心的优势。

然而福州城却无险可守。有句古谚形容福建上四府的形势：铜延平，铁邵武，豆腐建宁府，纸褙福州城。意思是说南平和邵武地形险要，固若金汤；建瓯像豆腐，早早投降算了；福州是纸糊的城市，不堪一击。最后这句还带点写实，旧时福州到处是连片的木房，板壁缝隙往往用纸张裱糊，一把火就会烧个干干净净。质诸古史，果然是这样，闽越国、闽国、明初陈友定割据，都不成气候。

福州迟迟不能确立自己作为文化中心的位置。宋代，福建的文化和学术中心在闽北，福州进士虽多，却很少有学术建树，就连附近的莆仙也比它牛气。到了明中叶，闽北文化和莆仙文化相继衰落，没想到闽南突然间人文蔚起，声势之盛，一点不让闽东。这似乎是一场福建各区域接力与省会城市进行的文化竞赛。

福州最后还是无可争议地成为了福建的文化中心。清乾隆年间，厦门港衰落，导致闽南经济和文化衰退，而福州则欢天喜地迎来了一个科举盛世。这也许是1707年省城创建的鳌峰书院有了出人意料的成果。有清一代，闽县、侯官两县考取的进士，占全省总数的40%左右。科举盛况还带来了文化的繁荣，一大批高官显宦和名流才俊，在事功和学术上均有建树，例如林则徐、沈葆桢、林旭、严复、林纾等，都曾经站在历史的潮头，深刻地影响着中国的现代化进程。

这里所提到的几位近代福州名人，都在三坊七巷住过。福州古民居最有人文意蕴的，当然是市中心的三坊七巷。这片古街区始建于五代，一千年了，不过今天的遗存多半来自明清，总共200多座建筑。我们欣赏古民居，见到一座两座精品，已是万幸，谁敢奢望整片古代街区完整展现在我们面前呢？更何况其中不少是耳熟能详的名人故居！人们不必计较它已经破败，走在窄窄的石板巷道上，粉墙黛瓦，曲线山墙，坊门跨巷而立，仿佛旧日时光重现。

三坊七巷的房屋门面都很朴实，不事张扬，与闽北大宅的雕花门楼无法相比。走进去，才知道其中另有天地，厅堂布局森严，高大开敞，不失官宦人家的气派。庭院的布置匠心独运，一个六角亭，一株荔枝树，一片假山石，都安置得停停当当，意趣盎然。其内部装饰的重点，似乎在于隔扇、窗棂、栏杆等细部，精雕细刻，毫不含糊。

福州长期作为国都、州治和省城，福州人变得儒雅、规矩、精明。明万历年间的《福州府志》说："其俗尚文词，贵节操，多故家世族，君子朴而守礼，小人谨而畏法。"大量福州人通过科举走上仕途，进入历代王朝的官僚体制，从而形成一种注重礼仪正统保守的文化传统。福州古民居与闽南古民居正好形成有趣的对比：前者注重经营建筑的内部，门面刻意低调，表现了福州官宦文化的谨慎；后者特别讲究建筑的门面，内部反而不大在乎，体现了闽南商业文化的张扬。一个图实惠，一个要面子。

闽东虽然临海，却是临海的山区，一点不亚于闽西北。闽东的山，往往被海水洞穿心腹；闽东的海，则陷入了群山的重围。海岸线就在山与海的贴身肉搏中回肠九曲，迂回往复。美则美矣，却成了交通的难题。福州与京城的联系，本来取道闽东到温州、台州最为便捷，结果因为畏惧险阻，改走闽北出境。闽东变成死角。

706年，长溪县（县治在今霞浦）的薛令之为福建夺得了第一个进士。薛令之的故乡福安廉村，诗书传家，历代在科举上都有所斩获，至今还保留下数十幢明清时代的宗祠和豪宅。然而，闽东地区开发虽早，发展却比较迟缓。由于缺乏经济腹地，沿海也无法形成重要商港，只能依靠渔业捕捞，山区依然是传统农业，自给自足。

闽东古民居，给人最强烈的视觉特征是弯曲的风火墙。闽北古民居的风火墙是阶梯状的，线条硬朗，气韵沉雄。闽东各地的风火墙是曲线的，优美生动，随着屋顶的高低而起伏，当地人称马鞍墙。它们更像两条腾飞的龙，勾勒出建筑的左右边界，翘首栖落在宅门两侧。前面说过，福州人对建筑的外表不太重视，低调从简，但惟独对风火墙特别热衷，宅门两侧的山墙排堵，泥塑彩绘，颇费心思去装饰。俯瞰福州老城，黑压压的一大片瓦房，无数条粉白的风火墙波浪般起伏，仿佛万马奔腾，千龙竞渡。

一张完全静态的民居画面，竟让人感觉风生水起，马嘶龙吟！我们说福州古民居含英咀华韬光养晦，然而忍不住偶尔露峥嵘。飞翔的风火墙，也许就是福州人鸿鹄之志的象征吧。

闽南古民居：鲜艳的红砖大厝

闽南古民居的风格极其鲜明，令人过目不忘。乍看，会让人惊叹：怎么每幢房子都像座小庙！闽西北古民居的屋脊是平直的，只有庙宇和宗祠才有弧形屋脊，檐角高翘。然而，所有闽南古民居的屋脊都弯成弧线，有的呈马鞍状，有的是两端斜入高天的长燕尾形。

闽南古民居的另一个特点是红砖红瓦，特别俗艳。这是很奇怪的。中国各地的民居，都以青砖灰瓦为主，不但因为青砖的质量优于红砖，还有建筑制度上的原因。红色是高等级建筑才能使用的颜色，例如皇宫和寺庙。闽南古民居

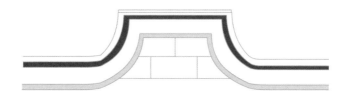

不但铺红瓦，还使用红色筒瓦，的确是僭越了分寸。

　　闽南人自豪地称他们的房子为"皇宫起"，也就是皇宫体的民居。有个民间故事解释了这种建筑样式的来源：闽王王审知的王后黄惠姑是泉州人，每到连绵阴雨天气，往往伤心落泪，闽王问她为什么。王后说她想起了娘家房屋破漏，不能阻挡风雨。闽王当即说："赐你一府皇宫起。"圣旨传到泉州，民众误以为泉州一府都可以建皇宫式建筑，遂大兴土木。有人密告闽王，说泉州人到处建皇宫，准备谋反。闽王想起是圣旨有误，连忙下旨停建，可是泉州晋江一带的房屋都已经建好，只好算了，圣旨传到南安地界时，南安的屋顶仅砌了三槽筒瓦，奉令即停。这样，南安的皇宫起大厝便保留下一个鲜明的特色，屋顶仅在两边砌三槽筒瓦。

　　闽南古民居的结构都差不多。普通的面阔三间，称"三间起"，中间为厅堂，左右各有一间房。屋脊要么用马背脊，要么用燕尾脊，都是中间凹陷两端微翘的优美曲线。燕尾脊更正式，翘得高昂，尖细，有轻灵飞动之势。大一点的是"五间起"，面阔五间，在"三间起"左右各加一开间，屋顶再多出两条燕尾，仿佛一大一小两双翅膀在低空飞翔。闽南的大户人家一定要建院落。前落是门厅，后落是主屋，再加上左右两排护厝或廊庑，团团围着一个天井，形成一个紧凑密封的合院。最典型的闽南大厝，如漳州蔡竹禅故居，就是三进双护厝。南安蔡氏古民居群，面阔一般为五开间，两进或三进，左右带一排或两排护厝。

　　红砖红瓦成了闽南建筑的独特视觉特征。在亚热带的强烈阳光下，碧海边，龙眼树与荔枝林的绿荫间，一幢幢鲜艳的红砖大厝显得特别明净亮丽、优雅动人。闽南人喜欢红色，也许与他们喜欢张扬和热闹的性格相关吧。

　　通常说的闽南，指的是原泉州、漳州两府的辖地，现在则分属厦门、泉州、漳州三市。从地理看，闽南地区有三个重要的特点。首先，它是福建最炎热的地区，临近北回归线，终年花果飘香。其次，闽南有漫长的海岸线，厦门干脆就是个海岛，面向世界的海洋对于闽南文化有决定性的影响。第三，闽南拥有福建四大平原中的两个，宽阔平坦，交通方便，语言相通。闽南是福建的精华所在。

　　闽南地区属泉州开发最早，宋元时代已成为整个东方世界最大的海港，是海上丝绸之路的起点。明代泉州港衰落，然而漳州的月港在明后期崛起，继续保持闽南人的航海优势。明清之际，郑成功一度控制了南中国海的海权，并从荷兰殖民者手中收复台湾。这是大航海时代欧洲殖民势力在全世界范围内遇到的一次重大挫败。清初，月港衰败后，它下游的厦门港横空出世，成为闽南地区的最大出海口。通过厦门，闽南人源源不断移民台湾和南洋。

　　闽南人的主体也是北方汉族移民，熟悉的是耕作农业，随着泉州平原的开发，部分人口开始往更南的漳州以至粤东潮汕地区迁徙。唐宋时期，漳州平原

还地广人稀，一片田园牧歌。明代闽南人多地少的矛盾日渐激化，沿海居民遂铤而走险，扬帆出海，开展海上走私贸易。明初厉行海禁，海上贸易具有违法性质，官府称之为海盗；明后期开放海禁时，海盗摇身一变，成了海商。闽南人走向海洋，是在官府打压的情况下进行的，亦商亦盗。这也使闽南人勇于冒险的性格得到强化。

海外贸易带来的巨大财富和宽阔眼界，造就了闽南文化迅速崛起。施鸿保《闽杂记》说："明时，兴化、泉州科甲之多，乡试每占通省之半。"兴化军是宋太平兴国四年（979年）从泉州分出去的，深究起来属于闽南文化系统。宋代莆田、仙游两县的人才超过福州、泉州这些大府，自成一军。明中叶以后，闽南与福州相比，无论科举人才还是学术成就，都有后来居上的势头。泉州的晋江、漳州的漳浦涌现了蔡清、陈紫峰、黄道周、蔡世远等一批著名学者，成为闽学重镇。文学上，福州的"闽中十才子"尊唐，闽南地区的文人多半反对，王慎中另开宗宋一派针锋相对，自创晋安诗风。

地域差异导致的文化差异很有意思。在民间，人们也经常认为，闽南人与福州人性格完全相反，互不买账。我有个朋友开玩笑说："福州人叫线面，闽南人偏偏要倒过来称面线；福州人说煎海蛎，闽南人就说海蛎煎。反正事事要反着来。"林鸿尊唐，王慎中偏偏要宗宋，也有点反着来的意味。

清中叶后厦门港衰落，闽南文化滑坡，福州无可争议成了全省的文化中心。不过，闽南与福州之争并未落下帷幕。20世纪末，闽南经济已经远远超过闽东，这是否意味着闽南文化即将复兴，并重启两地五六个世纪以来的文化竞争，还未可知。

民居的形态往往反映人民的性格。闽南人是晚近挟巨大的商业财富崛起的，年轻气盛，踌躇满志。起建豪宅大厝，是他们炫耀家族社会地位的一种方式。福州人那样讲究内部装饰，在闽南人看来是锦衣夜行，浪费银子，他们认为最重要的应该是建筑的外观。闽南地区盛产石材，好的建筑一定大量使用石料，看上去能传诸久远。高翘的屋脊很神气，红砖红瓦喜庆，他们拿来就用，全不管是否合乎礼制。

闽南古民居的装饰重点是门面。石雕、砖雕、镶嵌、瓷塑什么都往门楼上堆积，满满当当，花花绿绿，成为民间工匠展示才艺的场所。我去龙海石码看杨家大厝，还未进门，就被门墙上的各种装饰吸引了，使劲拍照，那真叫精美。如果是新建的门楼，你可能觉得俗不可耐，时间一久，再俗丽光鲜的事物也会沉静下来，变得雅致。我的胶卷已消耗大半，还没进门呢。没想到转进厅堂一看，已没什么可拍的了。

闽南建筑的屋脊装饰特别丰富。大约他们觉得这么显眼的位置闲着可惜，于是发展出泥塑、剪粘和交趾陶的技术，弄一排栩栩如生的神仙人物站在那里，五彩缤纷，煞是好看。屋顶垂脊正前方的牌头，什么亭台楼阁、鸟兽虫

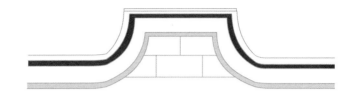

鱼、花果器具，都往上面堆垛，像满族妇女盛妆时满满当当的头饰。

很可惜，闽南本土现在已经很少见到这种刻意经营屋顶的建筑了。前些年我到马来西亚的槟城参观龙山堂，一座保存极其完好的闽南宗祠，首先就被它屋顶的豪华装饰震撼了。回国后我对曲利明说："我们在闽南采访过那么多闽南建筑，我告诉你，我见过的最好的闽南建筑在马来西亚。"

闽西古民居：有永久居民的碉堡

客家是最迟入闽的一个民系。到了宋代，福建大部分地区都已经被开发了，只留下偏僻的崇山峻岭。客家人从赣南一带进入福建的宁化、长汀，就此定居下来。

传统所说的闽西，是指古汀州府管辖的八县。从地理上看分为两片，北片是闽江支流沙溪的上游地区，如宁化、清流、明溪和连城，与闽北、闽东联系较密切；南片是汀江流域的长汀、武平、上杭和永定，汀江流入广东，与粤东北有较多的互动。客家人最早进入闽西的北部，因为东部早已被闽北人开发，更多的移民只好继续往南迁移，然而不久他们又遇到闽南人的阻挡，被迫往西沿着汀江出闽，进入广东。所以客家人聚集的区域多在赣南、闽西、粤东。

闽西是客家人关键的一站，不少学者认为，客家人正是在宁化、长汀落脚后，凝聚起族群意识，形成一个独特的民系。

"汀，山多田少，土瘠民贫。"宋代的《临汀志》说。闽西的自然条件不好，否则早就被更早的汉族移民占领了。后来为客，面对当地土著居民，宋以后的这批汉族移民自称客家。由于文化和人口优势，他们很快反客为主，成为闽西的主人。

落后的经济影响了闽西文化的发展。北片闽江流域的几个县，受闽北文化和闽东文化辐射，相对比较发达。唐代宁化就出过一个进士，宋代又诞生过郑文宝这样的名诗人。然而，直到明清之际，闽西才出现第一批在全省乃至全国有影响的人才，例如文人李世熊、黎士弘，书画家上官周、黄慎、伊秉绶。特别值得一提的是，宁化和连城两县涌现了阴承方、雷鋐、童能灵等重要理学家，当福州学风转为朴学后，他们还在从容不迫地研究朱子理论，支撑闽学残局。

客家人是一支长途跋涉辗转迁徙的民系，具有特别强烈的宗族意识和正统观念。这很容易理解，越是远离故土，越是需要团结，需要血缘与文化的认同。体现在建筑上，就是聚族而居，讲究礼制传统。客家人特别热衷于宗祠的建设，有大宗祠、小宗祠、房系宗祠等等，形成一个宗祠体系。看上杭的李氏大宗祠，那规模气势，让我们感动于客家人慎终追远的情怀。地形再不利，他们也要按中轴线起造大厝，为的是取中，给祖先的神主牌留个最好的位置。被称为"太师椅"的围垅屋，随山就势，导致后屋高出正厅，这本来不大妥当，但因为建筑结构保证了中堂坐落在中心位置，就有了可以接受的理由了。至于

圆形土楼，众望所归的圆心，必定建造一个公共祖堂，好一起祭拜列祖列宗。

客家人移民较晚，南方膏腴之地已经尽属先前的移民，只好深入山区，与土著居民进行种种争夺，斗争十分激烈。客家地区随处可见的土楼和围屋，反映了这一历史进程。

土楼是最具特色的闽西南民居。它们太独特了，与其他传统民居形成较大的差异，人们往往将它们单独论列。土楼，我们不妨视之为有永久居民的碉堡，一般建成圆形或方形，外墙用生土夯筑，厚实高大。闽西北也筑土墙，我自己就干过这活，手掌起过好多血泡。然而看过闽西土楼后，人们不得不佩服，打土墙的本领还是客家人厉害。在永定、平和寻找土楼的过程中，不时看见路边荒野立着几面孤零零的土墙，几乎完好无损，而房屋的木构部分却早已荡然无存。那些倔强的土墙像是永不瞑目的幽灵，要站到地老天荒。

那年正月，蒙蒙细雨，我们曾在永定的振成楼住过一夜。三楼，房间很小，有些潮湿，厕所在土楼外，所以天黑后就放个马桶在内圈廊道上。土楼内的住户大多数搬走了。深夜起来吸烟，一走动，廊道上的木楼板就发出响亮的咯吱声，似乎还有回声。四周静悄悄的，楼下祖堂剩下一个模糊的轮廓。土楼的大门都已关上，看不见星空，居住在土楼里的人像是安全地蜷缩在蛋壳里，或是子宫中。

客家区有一种被称为"九厅十八井"的大型民居，意思是有九个厅堂、十八个天井、上百个房间。连城培田的继述堂就是如此布局的，主体建筑是四进院落，左边一排右边三排横屋，共有18个厅堂、24个天井、72间房屋。培田还有幢叫"官厅"的建筑，结构更严谨，前塘后阁，中央五进院落，左右各带一排横屋。这种大型民居，是为了满足超大家族居住的需要而建造的，福建其他地方也有，但闽西地区最常见。聚族而居是汉族人的习惯，只是客家人特别重视而已。

生活在艰苦的闽西山区，形成了客家人朴实、坚毅的性格，漂泊与迁徙的族群经验，又使他们勇于闯荡，适应力强。例如同属农业社会，闽北人安土重迁，保守知足；客家人习惯于背井离乡，追寻新的生存空间。闽西的大山困不住他们。到了清代，客家人终于来到海边，毫不犹豫地远涉重洋，移民海外。被迫迁徙是一种苦难，然而深刻的迁徙记忆，对一个血气方刚的族群来说，也是一种财富。

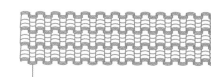

FUJIAN PEOPLES AND THEIR PREFACE

A large northwestern Fujian house that I lived in ——————————

When one talks of one's home village, or rather of one's homestead, one is referring first of all to the house one used to live in. I spent my childhood in a valley in northwestern Fujian. The village is a strip spread out along the foot of a hill and facing undulating paddy fields. A small brook winds through the village. On the opposite side, standing tall and upright, is the rugged Red Rock Mountain, as well as layers of distant mountains. My earliest and strongest memories come from an old house, sooty from the kitchen smoke—the Xiao family home.

I have also visited numerous villages in all parts of Fujian, where I have seen similar scenes. Concealed in every valley is a village where a clan lives together, building houses much the same as the Xiao family home. I feel completely at home in these other villages.

The Xiao family home is representative of traditional houses in northwestern Fujian, with a mountain in back covered with ancient tall trees. The front of the house looks out on open land, a well, a pond, and paddy fields. An expert told me that this was determined by fengshui. The large house, surrounded by a firewall, has two rows of buildings that are divided into five rooms. The larger middle two rooms serve as halls. Outside the firewall, on each of the left and right sides is another row of rooms. The courtyard is the center for ventilation and light in the house. Water from all four sides of the roof falls here: the people call this "four waters gathering in the center." The political core of the home is in the high, spacious main hall, where there is a shrine for sacrificing to the Xiao ancestors. Important ceremonies, such as ancestor worship, weddings, or funerals, all take place in this hall.

I often need to explain to people that in traditional Chinese homes, the quick and the dead live together, and the deceased take precedence. The most important place in a house must be given to the ancestors. Why are Chinese structures built carefully along axes? Because this is the way that people can decide where the most important places should be: in the center and higher.

The Xiao family is a large clan which has flourished over the years. After the division of the family, one or two rooms, including a hall, went to each nuclear family. Because the resulting space was limited, the people built additional houses in the vicinity. At the end of the 20th Century, when I went back to my old home, only two or three households were left there. Most people had moved to newly built brick houses. The Xiao family home, where a clan had lived in affection for two or three hundred years, had now been abandoned. In a short twenty-year span, the old house now had one foot in the grave. Because dozens of families had property rights to this ancestral home, it was impossible to make any changes: the fate awaiting her was continuous ruin, decay, and collapse.

This is also the fate of most of the traditional houses today. Our lifestyle has changed greatly, and traditional construction can't easily satisfy the many demands we make of our housing. In a rapid retreat from the stage of history, these old houses are being demolished or abandoned. This is the first time in the last few thousand years that only a few of them will be preserved as examples of cultural relics; most of the traditional Chinese domestic architecture will completely vanish within half a century. It's as if history has been cut by a sharp knife.

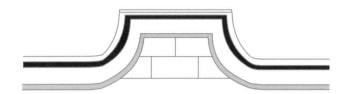

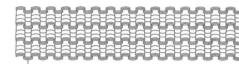

A large northwestern Fujian house that I lived in ——————————————

In order to understand the traditional domestic architecture of Fujian, one must first understand Fujian's geography, languages, and people. The architectural tradition is one part of the cultural tradition. It existed before we did, and yet it has changed because of us. People who emigrated from southern Fujian to Taiwan or Southeast Asia also built large red brick houses such as they once had in their homeland. When Europeans went to Gulangyu island in Xiamen, they imitated the western villa from thousands of miles away. But they were all changed to adapt to the geography and climate: new features were added and new styles gradually evolved.

Geographically, Fujian is known as the southeastern mountain land. Southeastern Fujian faces the ocean and Taiwan. The northeastern, northwestern, and southwestern regions all have high mountain ranges dividing Fujian from Zhejiang, Jiangxi, and Guangdong, thus forming a geographical unit. Mountains and hills occupy at least 80% of the land area. This is referred to as "80% mountains, 10% water, and 10% arable land." The two continuous 500-kilometer-long mountain chains paralleling the coastline – Wuyi Mountain on the northwest border and the Jiufeng-Daiyun mountain range in central Fujian – divide Fujian into the northwestern mountain region and the southeastern coastal region.

Most of Fujian's rivers, cutting through the mountainous northwest, flow southeast into the ocean, thus leaving a fragmented region in this area. The largest river, the Minjiang, has its sources in the northwestern Wuyi mountains. The streams converge in Nanping, and the Min then flows through Fuzhou and enters the ocean. It runs through the northern mountain region and the eastern coastal region. Several important rivers flowing through southeastern Fujian, such as the Mulan River, the Jin River, and the Jiulong River, have their sources in the central mountains of Fujian. These rivers are short, and their alluvial plains are rather wide and close to each other. The Ting River in western Fujian goes through Guangdong and enters the Han River. Western Fujian and eastern Guangdong together make up the Hakka region.

In general, Fujian can be divided into four regions: northern Fujian on the upper reaches of the Min River (the three ancient prefectures of Jianning, Yanping, and Shaowu); eastern Fujian on the lower reaches of the Min River and including the northeastern coastal area (the two ancient prefectures of Fuzhou and Funing); southern Fujian along the southern coast (the three ancient prefectures of Zhangzhou, Quanzhou, and Xinghua); and western Fujian in the southwestern mountain region (in ancient times, the Tingzhou prefecture), where the Hakka people live. Of course, we have to adjust these divisions a little. For example, Xinghua, now known as Putian and Xianyou, has been separated from Quanzhou since the Song dynasty. Their language and culture have their own special characteristics. People generally regard them as an independent region; seldom are they included in the concept of southern Fujian. In addition, geographically, Longyan and Zhangping should be part of southern Fujian, but today they are administratively part of western Fujian.

Fujian's languages are very complicated. In *Fujian Dialects*, Li Rulong divides Fujian into seven large dialect regions: eastern Fujian, represented by the Fuzhou dialect; Putian and Xianyou; southern Fujian, represented today by the Xiamen dialect; northern Fujian, represented by the Jian'ou dialect; central Fujian, represented by the Yong'an dialect; western

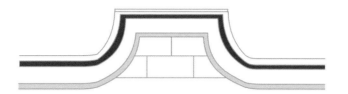

Fujian, represented by the Changting dialect; and northwestern Fujian and Jiangxi, represented by the Shaowu dialect. If we considered the central Fujian dialect and the northwestern Fujian dialect as variations of the northern Fujian dialect, the picture would be less complicated, for we would then be left with only the northern, eastern, southern, and western Fujian dialects, as well as the Putian-Xianyou dialect. The regions of the Fujian dialects would then essentially correspond with the geographical divisions.

The differences in dialects generally are predicated on the differences in peoples and cultures. In *Fujian's Six Major Peoples*, Chen Zhiping divides Fujian people into six groups: the northern Fujian people, the eastern Fujian (Fuzhou) people, the southern Fujian people, the western Fujian (Hakka) people, the Xinghua people, and the Longyan people. Each of these groups created a different, distinct culture. For example, there were the Neo-Confucian culture in northern Fujian; the government officials' culture of eastern Fujian; the ocean culture of southern Fujian; the farming culture of western Fujian; the imperial examination culture of Putian and Xianyou; and the commercial culture of Longyan. The differences in cultures directly influenced the style of building in each place, thus engendering all kinds and styles of residences in Fujian.

The present administrative divisions have sometimes confused the distinctive regional cultural characteristics. In 1970, the new city Sanming was established in central Fujian by combining part of the northern region and part of the western region. It was then that people started talking of northwestern Fujian. In terms of geography, my ancestral homeTaining county belongs to northwestern Fujian. I often need to explain to my friends that northwestern Fujian was not a cultural concept in the past. Taining county and Jianning county were part of Shaowu prefecture. Jiangle county and Sha county were part of Yanping prefecture. All four belonged to the northern Fujian culture system. Ninghua county, Qingliu county, and Mingxi county—all part of Tingzhou prefecture—belonged to the western Fujian culture. When we talk of culture, we have to return to the historical times when the cultures were shaped.

From the time the Qin dynasty [221-206 B.C.] established the central Min prefecture, Fujian has been a separate administrative entity, with its borders changing little. At the same time, because of the high mountains everywhere, transportation and communication within this area were difficult; thus, each region was comparatively independent and developed separately. Beginning in the Han [206 B.C.-220 A.D.] and Tang [618-907 A.D.] dynasties, large numbers of northern Han people migrated to Fujian; northern Fujian, eastern Fujian, and southern Fujian opened up one after the other. During the 300 years of the Northern and Southern Song dynasties [960-1279], the northern Fujian culture was kindled. With Zhu Xi [1130-1200] as the representative figure in the process, Min learning propelled Fujian's culture to its zenith, symbolizing the profound thought of the ancient Chinese. In a 1000-year period, the eastern Fujian culture was relatively stable, but it exploded greatly after the middle Qing period, with "many notables coming from here during the late Qing dynasty." [Qing dynasty: 1616-1911] The Putian-Xianyou area distinguished itself by producing scholars from the Song to the middle of the Ming dynasty [Ming dynasty: 1368-1644]; in this, it continuously led the entire province. Unfortunately, in 1562 its capital was destroyed by the attacks of Japanese pirates, and it declined. Although Quanzhou was the main international port and cosmopolitan city during the Song [960-1279] and Yuan [1279-1368] dynasties, it was only during the Ming and Qing dynasties that its culture suddenly burst forth with the splendor of the ocean culture. Western Fujian opened

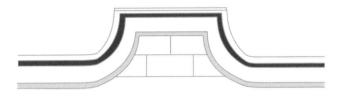

relatively late: not until after the Song dynasty did Han migrants move south in great numbers from Jiangxi. At that point, the distinctive Hakka people came into being. Their culture began to attract people's attention between the Ming and Qing dynasties.

It was also because of the fragmentation of Fujian culture that the traditional houses in Fujian became so rich and colorful. From northern Fujian's blue bricks and gray tiles to southern Fujian's red bricks and red tiles, and then to the circular earthen buildings of southwestern Fujian: what a sharp contrast this is! Other parts of China rarely have as many housing styles as Fujian. Of course, none of these housing styles came about accidentally: all have deep foundations in the people's lifestyles.

Traditional Houses in Northern Fujian: Beautiful Ornamental Carved Arches

The vast drainage basins of the three tributaries at the upper reaches of the Min River were historically divided into, and controlled by, the three northern Fujian prefectures. All the counties of the Jianxi's drainage basin were part of Jianning prefecture, with its government offices in present-day Jian'ou; all the counties of the upper reaches of the Futunxi drainage basin were part of Shaowu prefecture; all the counties of the drainage basin of the Futunxi's lower reaches and the Shaxi's middle and lower reaches were part of Yanping prefecture, with its government offices in present-day Nanping. The northern Fujian region is characterized by high mountains and dense forests. The rivers are rapid, and there is little flat land, but because it borders on Jiangxi and Zhejiang, it became the first stop for Han migrants into Fujian and thus it was the first to be opened up.

During the Han and Jin [265-420] dynasties, migrants began entering Fujian and settling down in northern Fujian. The men farmed and the women wove. They harvested crops in the fall and stored them for use in the winter. By the Song dynasty, the culture here had matured. Imperial examinations flourished and there were throngs of scholars, among them such notable personages as Zhu Xi, Li Gang, Yang Shi, Zhen Dexiu, Liu Yong, Yan Yu, and others. Most of the main figures in the so-called Min learning—Zhu Xi and his followers— were people from northern Fujian. They developed a major school—Min learning. With its profound thought and great influence, it stands as the zenith of Fujian culture. It has never been surpassed.

After the middle of the Ming dynasty, as a result of wars and other causes, the northern Fujian culture began to decline, but the depths of the Neo-Confucian tradition are still manifest in all its aspects. The solemnity and simplicity of the buildings in northern Fujian, the quintessence of restraint, show off the beauty of rationality and reserve. The many mansions of the rich and powerful are mixed in with ordinary alleys and roads. Only when you step inside and observe them in detail can you appreciate their deep meaning.

Taining's Shangshudi is one such example. It was the residence of Li Chunye, a defense minister in the Ming dynasty. It looks small and plain from the outside, and is wedged in with a large group of Ming and Qing buildings. Not until you walk into the corridor do you realize that this is a huge group of structures. Five buildings stand side by side along the corridor; each is divided into three sections. The buildings, independent of each other, are linked by corridors and side doors. The terse stone inscriptions, the rough beams and pillars,

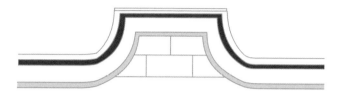

the vast courtyards: all embody the imposing atmosphere of Ming architecture. Most of the historic houses extant in Fujian were built in the Qing dynasty. Ming houses are rare. In its scope and its perfect preservation, Shangshudi is one of a kind.

A great deal of granite was used to build Shangshudi. In general, because it wasn't easy to quarry granite, people in northern Fujian were frugal in their use of stone for construction. It was placed in just a handful of spots, such as the doors, courtyards, verandas, and steps. Most of the comparatively stylish buildings in northern Fujian were constructed of brick and wood. More ordinary homes were built of earth and wood.

In the past, people in northwestern Fujian built their homes in a straightforward manner. First, they heaped up stone for the foundation. When they didn't have square stones, they used cobblestones from the river. They also needed tiles. Most important, though, they had to fell a lot of fir in the mountains. Fir is a special northern Fujian product; the trunks are straight and the trees are light and insect-proof, so it is an ideal construction material. An ordinary house can be built entirely of fir with no paint applied to it. On holidays, the walls are scrubbed with water, thus revealing the original beige color of the wood. Like a Song or Yuan dynasty painting, its texture is pleasing. After the wooden part of the building was constructed, the house was livable. If you wanted it to be a little stronger, during the slack agricultural season you could ask friends and relatives to help ram an earth wall to create a protective enclosure. If you could afford it, you could lay a brick wall, instead, and build a dazzling arch with beautiful, exquisite patterns carved into it. You could then flaunt this in the neighborhood.

The typical northern Fujian architecture was quite deeply influenced by the Anhui style: blue bricks and gray tiles, simple and tasteful. The ridges of ordinary people's houses are straight and flat, turning upward only at the corners of the eaves. The contour of the high wall undulates randomly, forming a step-like cadence. This modest structure, with its rigid outline and dark hue, calls to mind the traditional values of benevolence, righteousness, ritual, wisdom, loyalty, filial piety, chastity, and reverence. Northern Fujian architecture also has a luxurious element: the brick carving. Lifelike flowers, plants, birds, animals, immortals, people, and dramas were carved on the plain, dull, thick blue bricks. They were endowed with purity and elegance like black-and-white photographs. What impressed me the most was the archway built in honor of Lady Lian in Wufuli. That brilliantly and decoratively carved structure is mixed in with poor people's houses. It is as if an elegant aristocrat had been reduced to survive on the street corner. Now perhaps most of the exquisite brick carvings are preserved in Xiamei village in Wuyishan city. Several dozen arches of ancient people's homes show talent in carved decorations. At twilight one day, I saw the setting sun reflecting on the decorative engraved designs spread all over the arch of the Zou family's ancestral temple. They were as brilliant and beautiful as brocade.

The northern Fujian wood carvings are also splendid. Jinkeng in Shaowu has a building called Rulinlang. A row of six doors, as well as all the window casements in the wing-rooms, are carved all over with designs of flowers, birds, animals, and figures from dramas. The carvings are skillful, and the compositions concise and tasteful. This is the finest example of wood carving that I have seen in ordinary people's homes.

Unknown through the ages, the historic homes in northern Fujian are all quietly hidden in the villages. Once, Qu Liming and I found a small village called Wushi in Jian'ou. It was in the

wilds, and the path was tiny. We really didn't think there could be a village here. We didn't imagine that the village would actually have three old houses whose decorations were extremely exquisite. I gasped in admiration at the workmanship and patience of the Qing dynasty's artisans. The pillars' pedestals and caps, the supporting brackets on top of the columns, the window casements, the ornamental panels: all the decorative parts were worked on with special care. They are truly beautiful. The two caisson ceilings are extremely extravagant and showy. The murals and colored drawings remain lifelike and vivid. With the passage of time, the original thick ink and heavy colors have faded and become simple and elegant. A meaningful serenity has begun to emerge.

The owner wasn't present; a dog stretched out lazily in the main hall. Two children were walking around and talking. The old house reverberated with metallic sounds.

When we left, a woman at the end of the village said, "They're all dilapidated houses. Why are you interested in them?"

I said, "They're lovely. Partly because they are dilapidated. It's easy to build new houses, but not to create dilapidated ones."

An old house is not only mankind's creation, but it is also time's creation. Perhaps we can say that mankind and time have cooperated in creating it. But mankind alone cannot reach the core of the thing; it has to be washed by the time that is like a tide. Finally, the fake adornments flake away, and the core is unveiled. It is like the most abstruse ruptures in bare cobblestones.

Traditional Houses in Eastern Fujian: the Soaring Firewall

Eastern Fujian includes two parts: the Fuzhou area on the lower reaches of the Min River; and the ancient Funing prefecture (with administrative offices in present-day Xiapu) administering all the counties in eastern Fujian. Although both areas belong to the eastern Fujian dialect region, their geography, economy, and culture are all very different.

Fuzhou is located on the wide alluvial plain on the lower reaches of the Min River near the seaport. The land is fertile. On the east are high mountains that act as barriers against typhoons, but they don't keep the tides from reaching the city. The river and the sea meet here. Fuzhou's strategic position is extremely important. The famous Song dynasty official Cai Xiang explained it: "Fujian borders southern Zhejiang. Fuzhou can be reached by river in no more than two or three days from all the prefectures north and northwest of Fuzhou. On the eastern border is Wenzhou, and in the south Xinghua, Quanzhou, and Zhangzhou are on the seaboard. People from these prefectures can also reach Fuzhou by boat. Fuzhou is fundamental to all of these prefectures." Thus, it was natural for Fuzhou to become the main center of government in Fujian.

But, lacking natural barriers, Fuzhou was difficult to defend in wartime. An ancient proverb describes the strategic positions of Fujian's four principal cities: copper Yanping, iron Shaowu, beancurd Jianning, and pasted-paper Fuzhou. It means that Nanping and Shaowu were located in strategic places, and were strongly fortified; Jian'ou was like beancurd, and would surrender early; and Fuzhou was like pasted-paper lanterns, for it couldn't withstand even one attack. "Pasted-paper Fuzhou" was not just a metaphor.

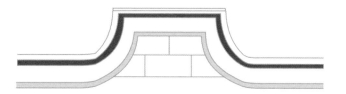

Everywhere in Fuzhou, wooden houses were connected together. Gaps in the wooden walls were patched with paper and paste. A spark would burn them all down. All the histories confirm this. The Minyue kingdom, the Min kingdom, and the separatist regime set up by Chen Youding by force of arms in the early Ming dynasty: none of them lasted long. When the central government's army moved in, Fuzhou fell in the blink of an eye.

Fuzhou was unable to establish itself early as the cultural center. In the Song dynasty, Fujian's center of culture and learning was in northern Fujian. Although quite a lot of men from Fuzhou passed the highest level of the imperial examinations, very few of them contributed to learning. Even nearby Putian and Xianyou surpassed Fuzhou in this. In the middle Ming period, the northern Fujian culture and the Putian-Xianyou culture both fell into decline. No one would have imagined that southern Fujian would suddenly flourish in the liberal arts. It didn't yield any prestige or influence to eastern Fujian. This was almost a regional relay, with all the areas in Fujian competing with the capital city.

Finally, Fuzhou became the indisputable center of Fujian culture. During the time of the Qing dynasty's Qianlong emperor [reigned 1736-99], Xiamen's port declined, thus leading to a waning of southern Fujian's economy and culture. At that time, Fuzhou moved toward its heyday in the imperial examinations. It was probably in 1707 that the capital city established the Aofeng Academy, the results of which exceeded people's expectations. During the Qing dynasty, 40% of Fujian men passing the highest level of the imperial examinations were from Min and Houguan counties in Fuzhou. The success in the imperial examinations led to a cultural flowering. A large number of dignitaries became high officials and well-known scholars. They all made achievements, as well as contributions to learning. For example, Lin Zexu, Shen Baozhen, Lin Xu, Yan Fu, Lin Shu, and others all stood at the crest of the historical tide, profoundly influencing the course of China's modernization.

The famous Fuzhou people from recent history mentioned here all lived in the "three lanes and seven alleys" part of Fuzhou. I studied and worked in Fuzhou for a few years, and felt that this city was somewhat unsystematic. But it has a special cultural beauty with historical traces scattered everywhere under the shade of the banyan trees. Of course, the Fuzhou homes with the most cultural significance are in the three lanes and seven alleys in the city center. Construction began in these old streets during the Five Dynasties period [907-960] more than a thousand years ago, though most of the more than 200 extant structures date from the Ming and Qing dynasties. We appreciate historic homes. When we see one or two exquisite examples, we feel very fortunate. Who could dare hope so wildly that an entire district of old streets could now be exhibited before our very eyes? How much more surprising that quite a lot of famous people's ancient homes are among them! I don't mind that they are dilapidated. As I walk down the narrow flagstone streets, I see whitewashed walls and black tiles, curved copings, and archways straddling alleys. It's as if the olden days have reappeared.

The houses in the three lanes and seven alleys all look simple on the outside. They are not showy. They can't be compared with the large houses with carved arches in northern Fujian. Not until you enter one do you realize that it's another world inside: the halls and rooms are high-ceilinged and spacious. They truly have the air of an official's residence. The courtyards were designed creatively and tastefully. A hexagonal pavilion, a lichee tree, and some rockery are all

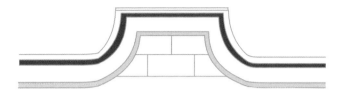

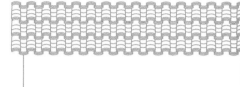

arranged perfectly and brim with charm. The interior decoration seems to focus on screens, window lattices, railings, and other delicate things. They were executed with great care.

Fuzhou has been the kingdom's capital and the provincial capital for a long time, and the people of Fuzhou have become refined, well-mannered, and astute. The *Fuzhou Chronicles* during the time of the Ming dynasty's Wanli emperor [1563-1620] says: "The common people esteem literature and honor moral integrity, there are many great old families, men of honor are simple and uphold the rites, common people are cautious and respect the laws." A large number of Fuzhou men passed the imperial examinations and had official careers. They became bureaucrats in imperial China, and thus shaped a cultural tradition that emphasized the rites and defended Confucian orthodoxy. Fuzhou homes and southern Fujian homes strike an interesting balance: the former give attention to the structure's interior while keeping the exterior low-key; this shows the caution of Fuzhou government officials' culture. The latter give particular attention to the exterior, and don't care much about the interior, thus showing the ostentation of southern Fujian's commercial culture. One focuses on substance; the other wants to look good.

Not until I went to Ningde in the late 1980s did I realize that although eastern Fujian is near the ocean, it is actually also in a mountainous area, just like being in northwestern Fujian. On the road from Ningde to Zhouning, I remember seeing two accidents. A large truck overturned and went over a frightening cliff. Most of the old houses in the vicinity of Zhouning have protective, enclosing walls built of earth. At the center of the front of each house is an upward curving arc. The ends of the eaves are slightly raised, like stylish women wearing soft straw hats. In 2007, I went to Xiapu. When the freeway went past the bay and through tunnels, I was surprised by the ruggedness of the eastern Fujian coastline. The eastern Fujian mountains often have caves created by the ocean water that go deep down into the mountains. Mountain ranges hug the eastern Fujian seaboard, and the coastline is the constant companion of both ocean and mountains, as if the mountains and ocean were engaged in a battle at close range that rages back and forth. It is beautiful, but it is a nightmare to drive there. To go from Fuzhou to Beijing, the shortest route is supposed to be via eastern Fujian to Wenzhou and Taizhou. But because of the danger, people began leaving Fujian from the northern part of the province, and eastern Fujian became a dead end.

In 706, Xue Lingzhi of Changxi county (the government seat was in present-day Xiapu), became the first man in Fujian to pass the highest level of the imperial examinations. In Xue Lingzhi's hometown of Lian village, there was a tradition of studying the Confucian classics. In each generation, some men succeeded in the imperial examinations. Now several dozen ancestral temples and homes of famous men from the Ming and Qing dynasties are still preserved. However, although eastern Fujian was opened up early, it was rather late in developing. Because it lacked economic resources in the interior, there was no way to establish an important harbor along the coast; it could only rely on fishing. The mountainous area was still a traditional self-sufficient farming area.

The most impressive feature of the ordinary people's homes in eastern Fujian is the curved contour of the firewall. I've said above that the firewalls in northern Fujian are shaped like ladders. Their rigid lines are sober and imposing. All of the firewalls in eastern Fujian

are curved and elegant. They rise and fall following the heights of the roofs. Local people call them saddle walls. I feel that they are even more like two flying dragons that rest at the two sides of the main entrance with their heads rising up. They outline the left and right boundaries of the structure. I've mentioned above that Fuzhou people didn't set much store by the exterior appearance of the structures: they are low-key and simple. Yet they also had high regard for the firewall. On the two sides of the door are clay sculptures and colorful drawings: a lot of thought went into these decorations. I've seen an old photograph of Fuzhou: there is a dense mass of tile houses, where innumerable whitewashed firewalls rise and fall like waves. They are also like thousands of galloping horses and dragons vying to cross the river.

    A still picture of the houses can actually make you feel the wind blowing and the water rising, horses neighing and dragons calling! We say that Fuzhou houses are modest and prudent; nonetheless, they are occasionally surprising in what they reveal. Perhaps the winged firewall symbolizes Fuzhou people's lofty aspirations.

Traditional Houses in Southern Fujian: Bright Red-brick Houses

    The style of the southern Fujian homes is very special and unforgettable. When I first went to southern Fujian several years ago, I was surprised: Every house is like a small temple! In northwestern Fujian, where my old home is located, the house ridges are flat and straight. Only temples and ancestral halls have curved ridges and eaves that are upturned at the corners. But the ridges of all of the southern Fujian homes are curved into arcs. Some are saddle-shaped; some are shaped like long swallows' tails on both sides and tilt toward the sky.

    Another characteristic of the southern Fujian houses is that they are built of red bricks and red tiles: they are really showy. This is strange. The houses all over China are built of blue bricks and gray tiles, not only because blue bricks are better quality than red, but also because red can be used only for high-grade construction--for example, for imperial palaces and temples. Yet, not only were red tiles used for southern Fujian homes, but red pantiles were also used. This really crossed the line.

    Southern Fujian people proudly call their houses "palace-like." A folk story explains the origin of this style of construction: the Min king Wang Shenzhi's queen Huang Huigu was from Quanzhou. Whenever there was a long stretch of overcast and rainy days, she wept brokenheartedly. When the king asked her why, she said that she was reminded of her home, which--dilapidated and leaky-- couldn't withstand the wind and rain. At this, the king said, "You can have a home like a palace." When his order reached Quanzhou, the crowds mistakenly thought that all of Quanzhou could build palace-style houses, and thereupon, they all engaged in construction. Someone leaked the news to the king, saying that Quanzhou people were attempting rebellion by building palaces everywhere. The king realized that his decree had been misunderstood, and immediately issued an order to stop construction, but houses had already been built along the Jin River in Quanzhou. Thus, he could do nothing. When the order reached Nan'an, the roofs there had just been laid with three rows of pantiles. They were ordered not to add any more. Thus, the palace-like houses in Nan'an county are distinguished by having only three rows of pantiles on each side of the roof; the rest of the roof is covered with regular tiles.

    The southern Fujian homes are all much the same. In general, there are three rooms—a hall

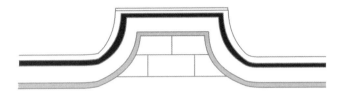

in the center and a room on each side. The ridges are sometimes horseback style, sometimes swallow's tail style. Both are sunken in the middle; the two ends are slightly upturned in elegant curves. The swallow's tail is the more usual style. Tapered and high, it looks as if it is flying. The larger five-room house has an extra room on both the left and right sides, and the rooftop has two more swallows' tails. It's as if two pairs of wings—one large and one small—were flying low. Wealthy families in southern Fujian had to build courtyards: in front of the courtyard is the hall; across the courtyard, the main rooms are in the back. On both the left and right sides, side rooms or corridors were built. Thus, all of these rooms formed a tight circle around the central courtyard. The most representative large houses in southern Fujian, such as Zhangzhou's Cai Zhuchan house, have three main sections and two additional side rows of rooms. The old Cai home in Nan'an is the width of five rooms. Whether the houses have two or three sections, the left and right sides each have one or two rows of side rooms.

The red bricks and red tiles became the characteristic features of southern Fujian architecture. Under the strong subtropical sun, beside the green sea, and in the green shade of the longan and lichee trees, all of the large bright red tile houses look young and beautiful, elegant and charming. Southern Fujian people's love of red may be related to their extroverted character.

The southern Fujian that we ordinarily speak of was originally the area governed by Quanzhou and Zhangzhou prefectures. Now it is divided into the three cities of Xiamen, Quanzhou, and Zhangzhou. Southern Fujian has three important geographical characteristics. First, near the Tropic of Cancer, it is the most torrid region in the province. Flowers blossom all year long. Second, it has a long coastline. Xiamen is actually an island. Facing the ocean, it has a decisive influence on southern Fujian culture. Finally, southern Fujian has two of the four largest plains in the province. With open, flat land, transportation and communication are easy, and the language is identical. Southern Fujian is the best place in the province.

Quanzhou was the first place to be opened up: in Song and Yuan dynasty times, it had already become the largest port in the entire eastern world. It was the starting point for the Silk Road of the sea. During the Ming dynasty, the Quanzhou port declined, but the Yue port in Zhangzhou grew in importance after the Ming dynasty, and carried on the seafaring superiority of the southern Fujian people. Between Ming and Qing times, Zheng Chenggong [Koxinga, 1624-62] once controlled the South China Sea and took Taiwan back from the Dutch. This was one time when the worldwide influence of the European colonizers during the great age of navigation suffered a setback. At the beginning of the Qing dynasty, after the Yue port declined, the Xiamen port on its lower reaches came into being and became southern Fujian's largest port. Going through Xiamen, southern Fujian people emigrated uninterruptedly to Taiwan and southeast Asia.

Most of the southern Fujian people are Han people who migrated here from the north. They were old hands at farming, and after opening up the Quanzhou plain, the surplus population moved farther south to Zhangzhou and Chaoshan. During the Tang and Song dynasties, the Zhangzhou plain still had a lot of land and a sparse population. It was a pastoral scene. During the Ming dynasty, the problem of too little land and too many people became acute, and the people living along the sea risked danger to go out to sea, where they became

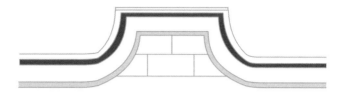

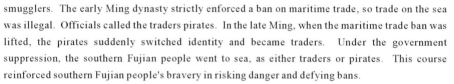

smugglers. The early Ming dynasty strictly enforced a ban on maritime trade, so trade on the sea was illegal. Officials called the traders pirates. In the late Ming, when the maritime trade ban was lifted, the pirates suddenly switched identity and became traders. Under the government suppression, the southern Fujian people went to sea, as either traders or pirates. This course reinforced southern Fujian people's bravery in risking danger and defying bans.

The great wealth and wider horizons engendered by overseas trade led to a swift maturing of southern Fujian culture. In Miscellaneous Recollections of Fujian, Shi Hongbao says: "In the Ming dynasty, numerous men from Xinghua and Quanzhou prefectures participated in the imperial examinations; the number accounted for half of those taking the provincial-level examinations." In 979, Xinghua was separated from Quanzhou. Although its culture was also rooted in the southern Fujian system, it grew too strong to remain a subordinate district. In the Song dynasty, there were more scholars in Putian and Xianyou than in Fuzhou, so a separate prefecture was established. After the middle of the Ming dynasty, comparing southern Fujian and Fuzhou, no matter whether in examination talent or in scholarly achievements, southern Fujian surpassed Fuzhou. Jinjiang in Quanzhou and Zhangpu in Zhangzhou produced a group of notable scholars—Cai Qing, Chen Zifeng, Huang Daozhou, and Cai Shiyuan. These towns became well-known in Min learning. In literature, Fuzhou's "Ten Talented Scholars of Central Fujian" respected the Tang, while most of the literary men in southern Fujian argued against this. Wang Shenzhong organized another faction that respected the Song. They were stern critics of Fuzhou's style of poetry.

The literary differences resulting from regional differences are interesting. People often think that the character of southern Fujian people is the opposite of Fuzhou people's character and that they don't respect each other. A friend of mine joked: "The same thin noodles that are called thread noodles in Fuzhou are called noodle threads in southern Fujian. The same dish that Fuzhou people call frying oysters, the southern Fujian people call oyster fries. The southern Fujian people purposely do everything just the opposite of the Fuzhou way of doing things." And so with literature: Wang Shenzhong upheld the Song style against Lin Hong's championing of the Tang style.

In the middle Qing period, Xiamen declined as a port, and the southern Fujian culture also waned. Fuzhou became the indisputable cultural center of the province. But this did not necessarily mean that the dispute between southern Fujian and Fuzhou had abated. At the end of the 20th Century, the southern Fujian economy far outpaced that of eastern Fujian. Does this mean that southern Fujian's culture is about to rebound, and that the competition between the two cultures will resume? We have to wait and see.

The style of houses often reflects the people's character. Southern Fujian people were late in starting to amass wealth from trade. Flourishing in their youth, they were complacent. Building grand houses was one way for them to show off their family's position in society. As they saw it, Fuzhou people's emphasis on elegant interior decorating was like wearing beautiful brocades for evening walks: it wasted money. They felt that the building's exterior was the most important. Southern Fujian is rich in stone, and the best structures utilized a lot of stone. They felt that stone made the houses look substantial. The raised ridges are stylish, and the red bricks and red tiles are festive. So they were adopted for the buildings with little concern for whether or

not they were appropriate.

　　The front of the building is the pivotal part of the decoration of southern Fujian homes. Stone and brick carving, inlays, porcelain figures: all were placed on the arches, so that they were covered all over with bright colors. They became the sites for the folk artisans to display their talents. When I went to see the Yang home in Shima, I hadn't yet entered when I was drawn to all kinds of ornamentation on the door and wall. I took lots of photographs. It is really exquisite. If it were a newly built arch, you would probably think it was incredibly vulgar. But because it is old, even gaudier and brighter things would become elegant. I used up most of my film before even entering the home. It turned out that not much inside was worth photographing.

　　The ridges of southern Fujian buildings are particularly richly decorated. People probably felt that it would be a shame for a spot that attracts so much attention to be unadorned. Therefore, they developed techniques for sculpting clay and using potsherds for colored pottery. They placed a lot of colorful little images of immortals standing in line along the ridges; these were very attractive. The front parts of the ridge corners are packed with designs of buildings, animals, flowers, and utensils, like the overly ornamental headdresses of Manchu women.

　　It's too bad that such painstakingly executed rooftops are now seldom seen in southern Fujian itself. A few years ago, I visited the Longshan hall in Malaysia. It's a southern Fujian ancestral hall that has been perfectly preserved. Above all, the elaborate ornamentation on its roof is thrilling. After returning to China, I said to Qu Liming, "We have visited so many examples of architecture in southern Fujian. But I tell you that the best example I've seen of southern Fujian architecture is in Malaysia."

Traditional Houses in Western Fujian: Permanent Blockhouses————

　　The Hakka were the last people to enter Fujian. By the Song dynasty, Fujian had already been mostly opened up, except for mountainous western Fujian. The Hakka entered Fujian from southern Jiangxi, and settled in Ninghua and Changting.

　　Western Fujian comprises the eight counties that were governed by old Tingzhou prefecture and is divided geographically into two parts. The northern part is on the upper reaches of the Sha River, a tributary of the Min. This includes Ninghua, Qingliu, Mingxi, and Liancheng; it is quite close to northern and eastern Fujian. The southern part comprises Changting, Wuping, Shanghang, and Yongding in the Ting River valley. The Ting River flows into Guangdong, so there is quite a lot of interaction with northeastern Guangdong. The Hakka people first entered the northern part of western Fujian, because the eastern part had already been opened up by the northern Fujian people. This new wave of migrants had to make their way continuously southward. But before long, encountering obstacles from the southern Fujian people, they were forced west along the Ting River. Some left Fujian and entered Guangdong. Thus, the Hakka people live in southern Jiangxi, western Fujian, and eastern Guangdong.

　　Western Fujian was an important relay station for the Hakka people. Many scholars believe that only after the Hakka settled in Ninghua and Changting did they become conscious

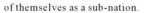

of themselves as a sub-nation.

　　"In Ting, there are a lot of mountains and not much land; the land is barren and the people poor," said a Song dynasty local gazetteer. Nature wasn't kind to western Fujian; otherwise, it would have been occupied by much earlier Han migrants. In relation to the indigenous people, this group of new Han migrants after the Song dynasty called themselves guests [Hakka]. Because of their superior culture and larger population, they quickly reversed their position and became hosts rather than guests. By either assimilating or destroying the people who had originally lived there, they became the masters of western Fujian.

　　The backward economy affected the development of the western Fujian culture. The counties in the northern part of the Min River valley were influenced by the northern Fujian and eastern Fujian cultures, and developed comparatively well. In the Tang dynasty, Ninghua produced one scholar who passed the highest level of the imperial examinations. During the Song dynasty, famous poets such as Zheng Wenbao appeared here. However, it was not until the period between the Ming and Qing dynasties that western Fujian had a group of men who were influential in both the province and all of China—for example, the literary figures Li Shixiong and Li Shihong, and the painters and calligraphers Shangguan Zhou, Huang Shen, and Yi Bingshou. Especially noteworthy were the major Neo-Confucian scholars from Ninghua and Liancheng—Yin Chengfang, Lei Hong, Tong Nengling, and others. After the Fuzhou scholars turned to textual research, these men persisted in working on the theories of Zhu Xi's disciples, thus bolstering the final phase of Min learning.

　　The Hakka people had been moving over long distances for a very long time. They had a particularly strong sense of clan relationships and respect for Confucian orthodoxy. This is easy to understand: the farther they went from their native land, the more necessary it was to have solidarity. They needed to identify with their blood and culture. This is embodied in their buildings, where the whole clan lived together and worshipped their ancestors. The Hakka were particularly fond of constructing ancestral halls for the whole clan and various levels of subdivisions of the clan. They have a complicated system of ancestral halls. The large Li clan ancestral hall in Shanghang is vigorous in scope. We are moved by the Hakka people commemorating their long-ago ancestors. Even if the terrain had been less advantageous, they would have made every effort to erect the main building on the central axis for a simple reason: to create a very central location for the ancestral tablets. The structure called "the armchair" was built on the mountain slope, and so the rear of the building is higher than the main hall. Normally, this wouldn't be very appropriate, but laying it out like this assured that the main hall was exactly in the central location. Thus, the design was acceptable. As for the circular earthen buildings, people had to build a public ancestral hall in the center, so that the whole clan could worship the ancestors together.

　　The Hakka people migrated too late, for the fertile land in the south was already occupied by other Han people. All they could do was go deep into the mountainous area and seize the indigenous people's last bastion. They had no choice but to do so by force. The struggle was very fierce. Reflecting this part of the history, everywhere in the Hakka area, you can see earthen buildings and blockhouses. From the mansion-style structures in the area of Changting and Ninghua to the Yongding-area earthen buildings whose main function was defense, this actually

represented a setback in architecture.

    Earthen buildings are the most characteristic houses in southwestern Fujian. They are unique, much different from the traditional house style. They are a genre all their own. We might as well think of the earthen buildings as blockhouses with permanent residents. Most are either circular or square. The outer walls, made of rammed earth, are thick, strong, high, and large. There are also earthen walls in northwestern Fujian. I've done this hard construction work myself. But after seeing the earthen buildings in western Fujian, I couldn't help but admire them. The Hakka were very skilled in building earthen walls. While I was looking for earthen buildings in Yongding and Pinghe, now and then I saw solitary earthen walls standing in the wilds beside the road. They were almost perfect and undamaged, and yet there was nothing left of the wooden part of the houses. Those stubborn earthen walls were like ghosts of people who had died with grievances: they would stand there for all eternity.

    It was drizzling in the first month of that year: I spent a night in the Zhencheng building in Yongding. Most of the residents of the building had moved away. On the third floor, the rooms were small and somewhat damp. The toilet was outside, so after dark, a chamber pot was placed in the corridor. When I got up in the middle of the night to smoke a cigarette, the wooden boards of the corridor creaked. It seemed there was also an echo. It was very quiet all around. When I looked downstairs, the ancestral hall could be seen only as a blurry silhouette. The main doors of the earthen building had all been closed. I couldn't see the night sky. It was as if I were coiled safely in an eggshell or in a womb. I was thinking: how could a group of Hakka living in a barracks-like house have maintained their privacy and developed their individuality? How much inconvenience and annoyance would they have had to deal with in daily life? People who always lived in a combat-ready state must have had very difficult lives.

    In the Hakka area a large house called "Nine Halls and Eighteen Courtyards" has more than 100 rooms. The Jishu house in Peitian, Liancheng county, is laid out like this. The main building has four sections along the central axis, and a row of rooms on the left side and three rows of rooms on the right side. In all there are eighteen halls, twenty-four courtyards, and seventy-two rooms. Another building in Peitian called Guanting is even more precise in its overall layout. There is a pond in front and a pavilion in back. In the center are five sections along the central axis, and each of the left and right sides has a row of rooms. Such a large-scale house was built in order to meet and surpass the needs of a large clan. Other places in Fujian also have houses like this, but they are most common in western Fujian. It's the custom of Han people to live in large groups; it's just that the Hakka people attach particular importance to this.

    Living in the difficult mountainous region of western Fujian has contributed to the Hakka people's simple, determined character. The clan's experience as vagabonds and migrants gave them the courage to make their living away from home and to adapt to new conditions. For example, both the northern Fujian people and the Hakka were farming societies. But the northern Fujian people were content with their lot and reluctant to move, while the Hakka were accustomed to leaving their native place and finding space for a new life. They couldn't be pinned down in the western Fujian mountains. During the Qing dynasty, the Hakka finally reached the coastline, and with great difficulty emigrated to places overseas. It was a trial to be forced to migrate, but the deeply etched memories of emigration are also a kind of spiritual treasure for a strong and courageous people.

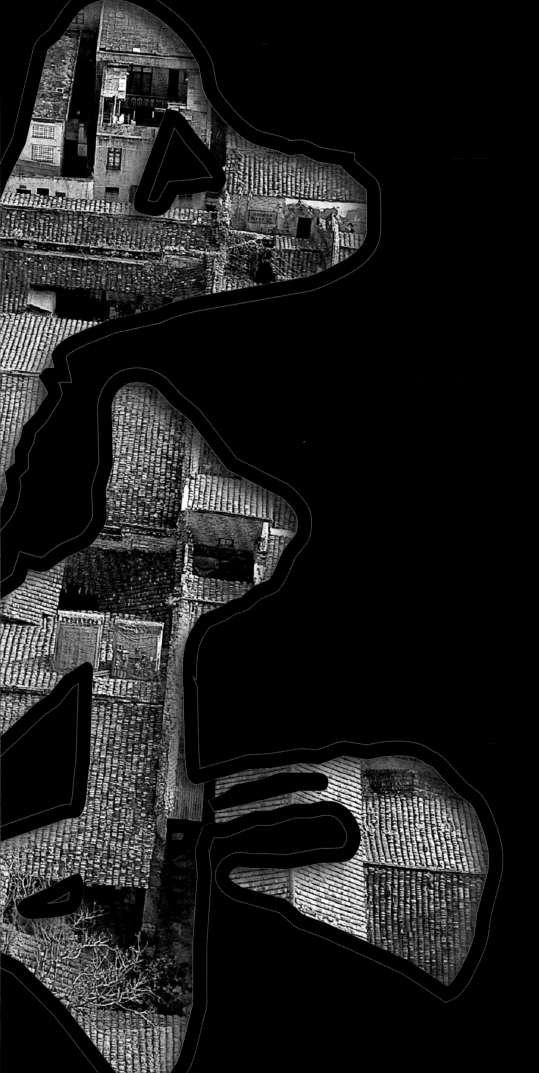

闽东古民居

闽东地区泛指福州市和宁德市所辖县市，流行闽东方言。

福州位于闽江入海口附近的冲积盆地，历代为全省政治中心，今天仍然是福建省会。同时，福州也是全省的文化中心，古迹斑斑，人文荟萃。

福州古民居通常门面端庄朴实，厅堂布局严谨，威仪气派，体现了官宦文化韬光养晦的特性。在院落中的亭台假山等小品的经营上，追求自然，流露出文人意趣。建筑的内部装饰，注重隔扇窗棂等木作部分，精雕细刻，工艺精湛。

三坊七巷是福州古民居的代表，白墙黛瓦，坊巷纵横，200多座明清建筑，以连片纵向多进式合院布局，其中不少是高官显宦和文化名人的故居，具有珍贵的历史价值。另外，闽清宏琳厝以规模宏大取胜，闽侯新坡古厝则以木雕精美著称。

宁德市的传统民居散落福鼎、霞浦、周宁、古田等县，往往夯生土筑曲线山墙。福安廉村因诞生了福建第一个进士薛令之而著名，同时，它还是一座城墙、宫庙、宗祠、民居等建筑元素都完整保存下来的古村落。

闽东古民居视觉上的最大特点，是高出屋顶的流线形风火墙，曲折多变，优美生动。

Traditional Houses in Eastern Fujian

The eastern Fujian region comprises the counties and cities administered by Fuzhou and Ningde. Eastern Fujian dialects are spoken here.

Fuzhou is located in the drainage basin where the Min River empties into the sea. It has been the province's government center for centuries, and remains the provincial capital. At the same time, Fuzhou is also the province's cultural center. It is full of historic and cultural sites.

The exteriors of Fuzhou people's homes are generally dignified and plain. The impressive halls are laid out precisely. They embody the modesty and prudence characteristic of the official culture. But the pavilions, artificial hills, and other ornamental features in the courtyards reveal the nature of literary men. In the interior decorating, attention was given to screens, window lattices, and other wooden components: these were painstakingly done, and the workmanship is superb.

The buildings in the three lanes and seven alleys are good examples of Fuzhou homes. They have whitewashed walls and black tiles. There are more than 200 Ming and Qing buildings, connected with each other. Quite a lot of them belonged to historic notables and famous people of culture. They hold rare historic value. In addition, the Honglin house in Minqing was built on a magnificent scale. And the historic Xinpo house in Minhou is noteworthy for its exquisite wood carving.

Ningde's traditional houses are located in Fuding, Xiapu, Zhouning, Gutian, and other counties. Generally, they are built of rammed earth and have curved contours. Liancun in Fu'an is a well-known village, because it produced Fujian's first candidate to pass the highest level of the imperial examinationsXue Lingzhiand because at the same time it perfectly preserves an entire ancient village, including the surrounding wall, temples, ancestral halls, houses, and other buildings.

The most impressive aspect of the eastern Fujian homes is the flowing contour of the firewall that extends high over the rooftops. The various curves are attractive in their elegance.

三坊七巷全景 / Panoramic view of the three lanes and seven alleys

三坊七巷（福州）

三坊七巷地处福州市区中心，占地约40万平方米，是唐末五代以来形成的千年坊巷。三坊是衣锦坊、文儒坊、光禄坊；七巷是杨桥巷、郎官巷、塔巷、黄巷、安民巷、宫巷、吉庇巷。现保存的实际只有二坊五巷，光禄坊、杨桥巷、吉庇巷均已改建为马路。

三坊七巷保存着200多座明清时代的建筑。在这片街区内，坊巷纵横，石板铺地，山墙曲折，黛瓦相连，深宅大院，雕梁画栋，是福州古民居的代表。尤其珍贵的是，其中包括林则徐、沈葆桢、林旭、林纾、严复、陈衍、谢冰心等一大批历史文化名人的故居。

The Three Lanes and Seven Alleys (Fuzhou)

The three lanes and seven alleys occupy 400,000 square meters in the center of Fuzhou. They date from the end of the Tang and the Five Dynasties and later dynasties, and thus are more than 1000 years old. The three lanes are Yijin, Wenru, and Guanglu; the seven alleys are Yangqiao, Langguan, Ta, Huang, Anmin, Gong, and Jibi. Actually, only two lanes and five alleys are extant.

More than 200 Ming and Qing buildings are preserved in the neighborhood of the three lanes and seven alleys. In this section of the city, the lanes and alleys intersect, flagstones are spread on the ground, the copings zigzag, black tiles are linked together, and the big houses are all beautifully decorated. They are representative of the historic houses in Fuzhou. Especially rare is that they include the homes of famous people in history and culture, such as Lin Zexu, Shen Baozhen, Lin Xu, Lin Shu, Yan Fu, Chen Yan, Xie Bingxin, and others.

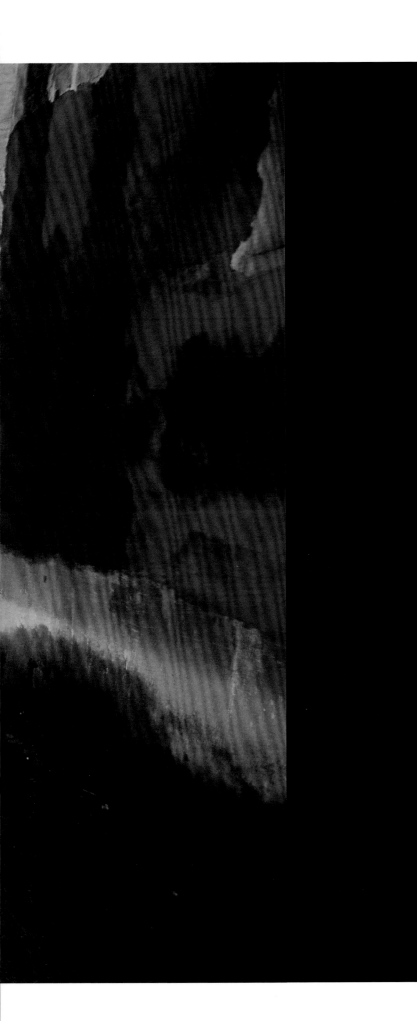

青石铺地的巷道 / An alleyway paved with blue stones

繁华总被雨打风吹去 / The bloom has faded long ago

连片纵向多进式合院鸟瞰 / Bird's-eye view of a house

夜幕降临，闽戏登场 / As night falls, Fujian opera is performed

牌楼跨巷而立 / Coping ornamentation

闽东古民居的内部装饰尤重木雕

The beauty of the interior decoration of eastern Fujian homes lies in the wood carving

门巷依然 / The lane

粉墙黛瓦 / Whitewashed wall and black tiles

古巷悠长，寂寞 / The historic alley: long and lonely

宏琳厝（闽清）

位于闽清县坂东镇新壶村，药材商人黄作宾于清乾隆六十年（1795年）始建，28年后，其子宏琳续建完工。宏琳厝占地面积1.7万多平方米，厝内廊回路转，纵横有序，共有大小厅堂35间、住房666间、花圃25个、天井30个、水井4口，号称全国最大的古民居。建筑为土木结构，对称冀券仰，雕梁画栋，工艺精湛，堪称民间建筑艺术的瑰宝。

The Honglin House (Minqing)

This is in Xinhu village, Bandong town, Minqing county. Construction on it was started in 1795 by the herbal medicine dealer Huang Zuobin; twenty-eight years later, his son Honglin finished it. The Honglin house occupies more than 17,000 square meters of land. Inside the wall, corridors and passages connect rows and rows of buildings. There are thirty-five large and small halls, 666 rooms, twenty-five gardens, thirty courtyards, and four wells. It is known as the largest historic home in China. It was constructed of earth and wood. The poles and ridges are beautifully decorated with carvings and paintings. The craftsmanship is superb. It is indeed a treasure of folk architecture.

宏琳厝气势非凡 / The Honglin House

大夫第 / Dafudi imperial official's residence

供奉祖宗神主牌位的神龛 / Shrine for worshipping the ancestors

厅堂 / A hall

回廊 / Cloister

巷道 / Alleyway

新坡古厝（闽侯）

位于闽侯县白沙镇新坡村，始建于清乾隆元年（1736年），占地面积达1万平方米，系江永奋、江永襄兄弟所建。古厝沿中轴线由南至北纵深向里排列5座，加上旁边两座，共计7座组成，出檐深远，气势恢弘。新坡古厝的木雕艺术尤其为人称道，插屏、门窗、格扇、斗拱、梁枋等，均精雕细刻，不施彩绘，精美绝伦。

The Old Xinpo Houses (Minhou)

Located in Xinpo village, Baisha town, Minhou county, these houses were first built in 1736, and occupy 10,000 square meters of land. They were built by the Jiang brothers—Yongfen and Yongxiang. Five houses are laid out north to south on the central axis. Along with two houses on the side, the complex comprises seven buildings. The eaves extend far from the buildings, and impress people with their vigor. Drawing special praise are the unpainted and carefully executed wood carvings on the screens, doors, windows, brackets, and girders. They are brilliant and exquisite.

全景 / Panoramic view

宽大的庭院 / The extensive courtyard

脊檐与山墙牌堵装饰 / Decorations on the ridge ends and copings

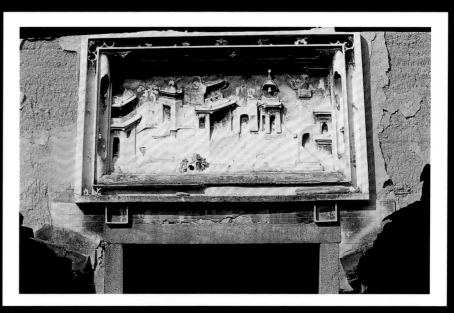

雕花栏板 / Carved pillar

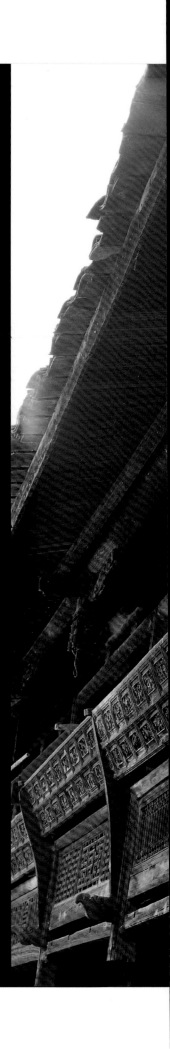

粗壮的梁柱，精巧的木雕工艺 / Fine carving on large girder

木雕饰品栩栩如生 / Vivid wood carving

雕刻精致的垂花柱 / A "hanging flower" pillar

翠郊古厝（福鼎）

位于福鼎市白琳镇，建于清乾隆十年（1745年）。整体布局以三座三进合院为主体，有6个大厅、12个小厅、24个天井、192间房、360根木柱。古厝内代表江南建筑风格的木雕饰品精美细致，所有的梁、柱、窗、门皆饰以木雕图案，或人物、或花卉、或祥禽、或瑞兽，栩栩如生。翠郊古民居保存较为完好，具有典型的南方山区建筑风格。

The Old Cuijiao House (Fuding)

Located in Bailin, Fuding city, this site covers 14,000 square meters, with the house occupying 5000 square meters. Construction began in 1745. It is laid out in three buildings, each of which has three parallel sections. The complex has a total of six large halls, twelve small ones, twenty-four courtyards, 192 rooms and 360 wooden pillars. Inside, there are exquisite wood carvings, typical of the southern China style. All the girders, pillars, windows, and doors have lifelike wood carvings of people, flowers, and auspicious birds and animals.

The historic Cuijiao house has been preserved quite well. It is typical of the architectural style in the southern mountainous regions.

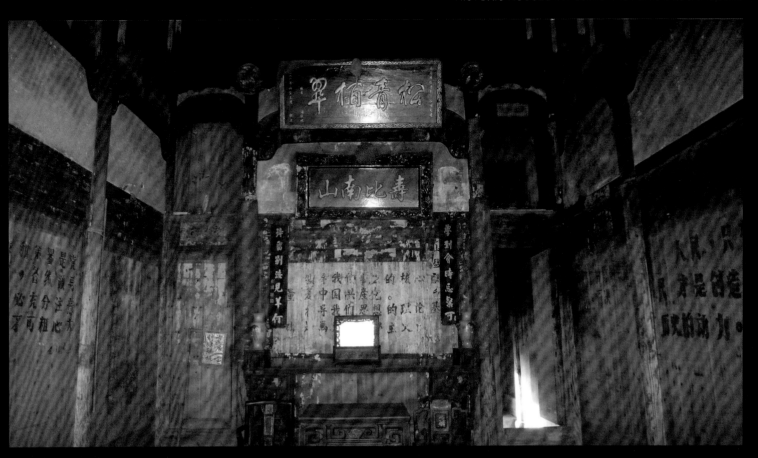

厅堂与庭院 ／ A hall and courtyard

二楼重檐 / Doubled eaves on the two floors

回廊过道 / Cloister

房屋之间侧门相通 / Side doors between the rooms

夕照下的杉木板材特别温馨 / Sunset glow on the fir materials

斜阳穿门入室 ／ Light from the setting sun shines in the room

藻井结构巧妙，装饰精美 / Beautifully decorated caisson ceiling

斗拱木雕工艺精湛，层叠有序 ／ Wood carving on brackets

雕饰图案展示了古厝的美学意蕴 ／ Girders, beams, and poles decorated with carvings and paintings

夕阳下的隔扇门窗 ／ Screens, doors, and windows under the setting sun

柱础石雕，稳当沉实 / Carving on a stone plinth

古墙老藤，一派沧桑之美／Old vines on an ancient wall

庭院居室，幽雅宁静／Courtyard and rooms show ancient taste

风车、水桶、磨盘见证了岁月的沧桑和乡村的变迁

Winnowers, water buckets, and millstones bear witness
to the changes in the village over the years

古床、橱柜，造型庄重，结构严谨，装饰华丽／An old bed and cupboard

廉村（福安）

　　位于福安市溪潭镇穆阳溪中游西岸，是福建第一个进士薛令之(唐神龙二年即公元706年及第)的故乡，被誉为开闽进士第一村。薛令之为官清廉，御赐"廉村"。1560年村民筑城墙以御倭寇，称廉村堡。廉村历代人才辈出，相当繁华，至今尚存三个城门，以及明清民居26座，清代祠庙4座。不少房屋还摆放着镂雕精致的家传大型木屏风。城东有明代古码头2座，曾是通往大海的内河港口，也是沟通闽东北和浙南的水陆枢纽和物资集散地。

Liancun (Fu'an)

On the west bank of the middle reaches of Muyangxi in Xitan town, Fu'an city, is the home village of the first Fujian man to pass the highest level of the imperial examinations, Xue Lingzhi. (He passed it in 706.) Xue Lingzhi was an upright official, and so his home village was called "Liancun" [Honesty Village]. In 1560, a rampart was built to keep the Japanese pirates out; it was called Liancun fortress. It used to be prosperous. Large numbers of scholars appeared in each generation. Three city gates are extant, as well as twenty-six homes from the Ming and Qing dynasties, and four ancestral temples from the Qing dynasty. Exquisitely carved wooden screens handed down through the generations still remain in quite a lot of the houses. East of the city wall are two wharves built in the Ming dynasty. The freshwater ports led to the sea, and served as a communications hub and distributing center between northeastern Fujian and southern Zhejiang.

古码头、古官道、古城堡是廉村历史最显著的见证／An old wharf, public road, and fort attest to Lian village's history

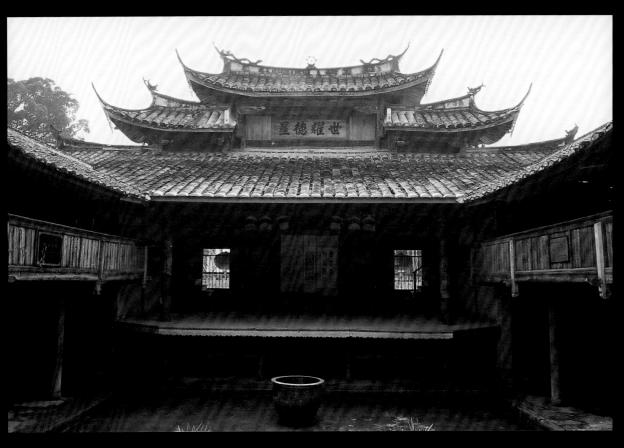

明清时期的宗祠、支祠、后湖宫、妈祖庙、古戏台迄今仍保存完好 / Ancestral halls, temples, and an old opera stage have been preserved from Ming and Qing dynasty times

鹅卵石铺就的古村道，缓缓延伸，通贯村落 / An old cobblestone road runs through the village

苍劲古树成了地域历史的丰碑／An ancient tree

雕镂精致的大型木屏风／A large carved wooden screen

庄重精致的供桌／Altar table

华丽的屋顶装饰／Rooftop decorations

苔迹斑驳的古碑石，尚存完好的石狮，记载着昔日的辉煌 / An ancient stele and a stone lion, recording the glory of the past

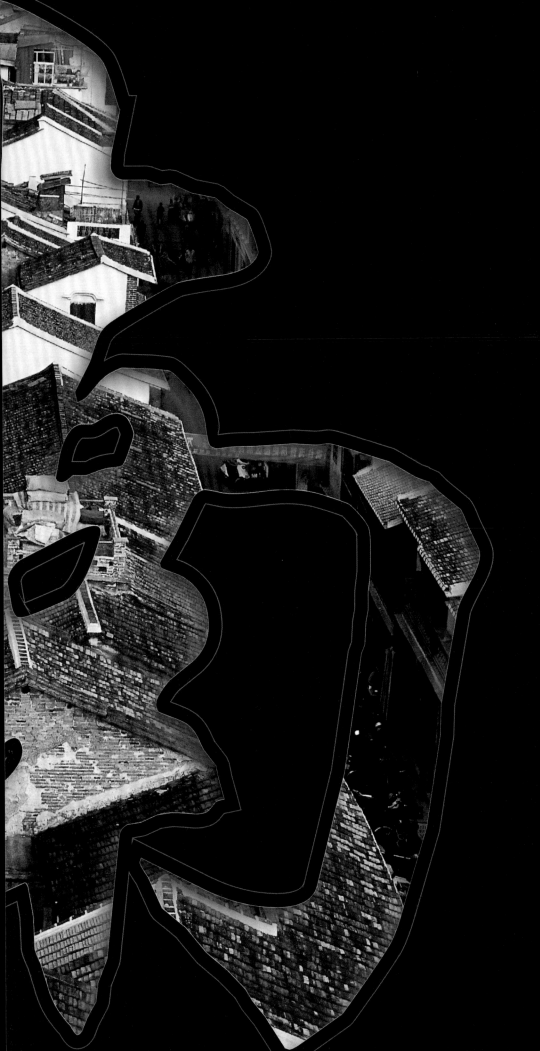

　　闽南地区习惯指厦门、泉州、漳州三市所辖县市。莆田、仙游宋代
从泉州析出，其建筑形态与闽南接近，附列本章。

　　闽南沿海有漳州和泉州两个小平原，气候温暖，土地肥沃，是福建
华所在。宋元时期，泉州为东方第一大港，是海上丝绸之路的起点；明
时期，闽南地区的出海口转移到漳州和厦门，闽南人继续保持海上优势
不但通贩东西洋，还大量移民台湾和东南亚地区。闽南文化具有海洋文
的特性。

　　传统的闽南大厝具有鲜明的地域风格：红砖红瓦，色彩鲜艳，屋脊
为优美的马背脊或燕尾脊。从结构看，大户人家的豪宅一般为三进院落
两旁各加一排或两排护厝，砖木结构。闽南地区盛产石材，因此台基、
身、石柱、门框、台阶、铺地等方面大量使用石料，并在关键部位精心
刻，形成独具闽南特色的石雕艺术。

　　闽南地区经济发达，古民居散落各地，毁损比较严重。漳州天宝镇
洪坑村、晋江的龙湖镇，还残余成片的红砖民居；南安蔡氏古民居建成
间较晚，是闽南地区保存最好的连片建筑群。莆田古民居与闽南古民居
属红砖系统，风格近似。仙游赖店镇的鸳鸯大厝气势宏大，雕梁画栋，
难得的精品。

Traditional Houses in Southern Fujian

The term Southern Fujian customarily refers to the counties and cities administered by Xiamen, Quanzhou, and Zhangzhou. Putian was separated from Quanzhou during the Song dynasty, but because its architectural style is close to that of southern Fujian, I am also mentioning it here.

Two small plains, the Zhangzhou and the Quanzhou, are located along the southern Fujian seaboard. Because of the warm climate and the fertile land, it is the best location in Fujian. During the Song and Yuan dynasties, Quanzhou was the major port in Asia and the jumping-off point for the Silk Road of the Sea. During the Ming and Qing dynasties, Zhangzhou and Xiamen became important ports in southern Fujian, and the people here continuously maintained their superiority on the sea. Not only did they engage in trade with the east and west, but also large numbers of people emigrated to Taiwan and Southeast Asia. Thus, southern Fujian culture is characterized by the ocean culture.

The traditional large houses of southern Fujian are noteworthy for their regional style: red bricks and red tiles, colorful and gorgeous. Most of the ridges curve like elegant horse backs or swallow tails. Most of the rich people's impressive homes are built of brick and wood. Most have three sections, with courtyards separating them. On each of the two sides are one or two rows of additional rooms. Southern Fujian is rich in stone, and so a lot of stone is used for the foundations, the body of the walls, the pillars, door frames, steps, and grounds. There are also exquisite carvings in key spots. All of this shaped southern Fujian's singular skill in stone carving.

Southern Fujian is a prosperous area. The historic homes can be seen here and there, but most of them are no longer in good shape. In Hongkeng village, Tianbao town, Zhangzhou, and Longhu town in Jinjiang, some neighborhoods of red-tiled homes still remain. The Cai family home in Nan'an was built relatively late: it is the best preserved group of buildings in southern Fujian.

Like the southern Fujian homes, the Putian homes are characterized by red tiles; the style is almost the same. The large Yuanyang house in Lai town, Xianyou, is vast and grand. With its carved girders and drawings on ridgepoles, it is exquisite.

邱得魏厝（厦门）

　　又称庆寿堂，位于厦门海沧新垵惠佐村。典型的闽南民居风格，约建于清道光中后期。房屋主人邱得魏是越南华侨，做大米生意发达后衣锦还乡，建了这座房子。庆寿堂前后三落，两旁护厝，前面晒埕外还有一排倒座。村里还有不少传统民居，邱得魏大厝的木雕最为精彩，梁枋、坐斗、瓜柱、屏门、格扇，均精雕细刻。第三落中厅的月洞落地罩，用荔枝木精心雕刻而成，漆金彩绘，在传统民居中极其罕见 。

Qiudewei House (Xiamen)

　　Located in Huizuo village, Haicang, Xiamen, this typical traditional southern Fujian home is also called the "celebrate longevity" hall. It was probably constructed late in the rule of the Qing dynasty's Daoguang emperor [1821-1850]. Its owner Qiu Dewei was an overseas Chinese living in Vietnam. Returning home after making a fortune in the rice business, he built this house. The Celebrate Longevity Hall has three sections separated by courtyards, and additional rooms on the two sides. Across from the threshing ground in front, a row of rooms faces the back. There are a lot of other traditional homes in the village, but the wood carving in Qu Dewei's large home is the most exquisite. The girders, pillars, and screens were all executed with great care. In the third section, the opening shaped like a full moon in the main hall's screen was carved from lichee wood; it has gold lacquer and colored drawings.This is rare among traditional homes.

古厝建有亭台楼阁，创造了自然的生活空间 / Old pavilion attached to the historic house

高低不平、错落有致的古厝 / An old residence

内架构简洁、对称 / The interior structure is symmetrical

庄严肃穆的神台供桌／A large altar table

雕刻玲珑剔透、金碧辉煌的祖先牌位 / Ancestral tablet

富丽堂皇、精致美观的厅堂门楼 / Archway over clan hall

雕刻精美的石鼓，突显大厝的威严 / A drum, beautifully carved from rock

柱础，高浮雕装饰／Stone decoration

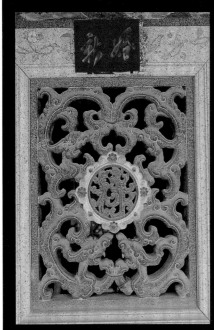

门面，是整个大厝的重要装饰部分，各种木雕、石雕、彩绘组成的图案光彩耀眼，目不暇接

A front door decorated with wood, stone, and plaster carvings, as well as drawings

门前装饰，各种工艺争奇斗艳，美不胜收／Decorations on the front door

"门当"也是工匠展示手艺的地方，其中高浮雕尤为精湛／The part above the front door also shows the skill in carving

施调赓故居（漳州）

位于漳州市新行街，是昔日本地区重要的商贸集散地。故居为街巷式建筑，窄而细长，人称"竹竿厝"；基本格局是三进"三堂三井"，两边风火墙高耸，与邻居共有。施宅98号，为清翰林施调赓故居，有花园假山水池，布局精巧，目前还保留较为完整的建筑形态。

The Old Shidiaogeng House (Zhangzhou)

This is located at No. 98 Xinhang Street in Zhangzhou city, a street which used to be an important commercial center in Zhangzhou. The streets are narrow and long, so people call it the Bamboo Pole House. It is typical of the homes having three sections.The layout is essentially "three halls and three courtyards." On both sides, the firewalls soar, and are shared with the neighbors. The Shi home, that of the Qing dynasty Hanlin Academy scholar Shi Diaogeng, has gardens, artificial hills, and ponds. The layout is refined. The house is quite perfectly preserved.

一条保存较为完好的闽南古建筑街巷，虽经
岁月的风刀霜剑，裂痕纵横交错，却依然红艳如
火，昭示着这里曾经的辉煌

A rather well-preserved old street in Southern Fujian

院内亭台楼阁 / A courtyard with pavilions

庭院清净淡雅 / A courtyard's simple elegance

"骑马楼"，闽南街道独特的建筑风格，楼上住宅，楼下商业旺铺，刮风下雨行走便利

"Horse-riding building": a construction style unique to Southern Fujian, with the second floor jutting out, protecting the sidewalk. The living quarters are upstairs, while the shop is on the ground floor

西洋雕塑，记录了当年中外交流的场景

Western sculpture shows the contact between China and the outside world

闽南古民居 — 蔡竹禅故居

The Historic Cai Zhuchan House (Zhangzhou)

Construction on this house, which is in Zhangzhou city, began during the time of the Qianlong emperor in the Qing dynasty. In the 1940s, the well-known businessman Cai Zhuchan bought it and engaged the famous artisan Li Mingyue to take charge of restoration. This was completed in 1948. A typical traditional home built in three sections with two rows of side rooms, it has a stone threshing ground in front, a garden in back, and the spacious halls and light courtyard covered with blue stone. The structure is perfect, the ornamentation beautiful. Probably because of the restoration, Cai Zhuchan's old home doesn't have the refined detail work that other traditional Qing dynasty houses have; nonetheless, it is grand, imposing, and aesthetically pleasing.

蔡竹禅故居（漳州）

坐落在漳州市区，创建于清乾隆年间，20世纪40年代著名实业家蔡竹禅购得，请名匠李明月主持重修，1948年竣工。典型的三进双护厝民宅，前有石埕，后留花园，庭院宽敞明亮，全用青石铺地，结构完整，装饰精美。可能是重修的原因，蔡竹禅故居不像其他清代民居那样精巧细致，但却显得雄浑大气，另具美妙。

在现代建筑包围中的古老大厝，依旧显露出古老的魅力

The charm of the ancient is still evident in the historic buildings which are surrounded by modern buildings

高墙围护着深宅大院 / A high wall surrounds the large courtyard and buildings

居住地的温馨，和谐 / The warmth and harmony of the residences

珍奇花草，布满房前屋后 / Beautiful plants everywhere around the house

屋内供奉着祖先的牌位 / Ancestral tablets

精美的梁柱，展示了古厝的辉煌 / Beautiful girders and columns

规尖上精美的灰塑 / Exquisite plaster sculptures

门楣、石鼓，造型独特，处处显示着石雕工艺的精妙绝伦 / Lintels and stone drums

寓意深刻的柱础石雕图案 / Carving on a stone plinth

蓝廷珍府第（漳浦）

　　位于漳浦县湖西畲族乡顶坛村，系清康熙、雍正年间福建水师提督蓝廷珍建造的府第，也是其孙江南水师提督蓝元枚的故居。府第始建于康熙末年，雍正五年（1727年）落成，朝东，面宽50米，纵深86米，占地约4300平方米。纵向五落，左右两厢为护厝，构成大四合院套小四合院的格局。四周建筑犹如城墙环绕，有院城之称。因为与赵家堡、诒安堡相邻，故俗称"新城"。

The Lan Tingzhen Mansion (Zhangpu)

　　This is located in Dingtan village in the minority She people's district of Huxi in Zhangpu county. This mansion was built by Lan Tingzhen, who was an admiral in Fujian during the early 18th Century. It was also the residence of his grandson, the admiral of Southern China's navy Lan Yuanmei. Construction began in the late Kangxi period [reigned 1662-1722] and was completed in 1727. It faces east and is 50 meters wide and 86 meters deep. It occupies a little more than an acre of land. There are five main sections, with side rooms on the left and right sides. On the four sides is a wall like a city wall. Because it is next to the Zhao family blockhouse and the Yi'an blockhouse, local people call it the "new town"

红砖红瓦配以坚硬的花岗石筑成的古宅，但见破旧的门板、树藤攀附着的墙体，虽经岁月风霜雨雪的磨砺，却依旧魅力无穷

An old residence built of red bricks and tiles and massive granite

杨家大厝（龙海）

　　位于龙海市石码镇霞庵路。1904年，侨居印尼的富商杨世泰回国兴建，两年后落成。典型的闽南单幢建筑，三间正屋，二进，左右各一排纵向护厝，配有后花园，总面积约1600平方米。杨家大厝面积不大，门楼却美轮美奂，精彩绝伦，石雕、泥塑、瓷塑、影雕镶嵌、剪粘，无所不用其极。很特别的是，装饰带有明显的南洋风格。

The Yang Family Home (Longhai)

　　It is located on Xia'an Street, Shima town, Longhai. In 1904, the wealthy merchant Yang Shitai, who had been living in Indonesia, came home and started construction on it. It was completed two years later. Typical of Southern Fujian structures, it has two sections, each with three rooms facing the courtyard. On the left and right sides of the courtyard are rows of side rooms. There is also a garden in back. The whole building occupies about 1600 square meters of land. Although the Yang home isn't large, its archway is superb. The stone carvings, clay sculptures, porcelains, and the pictures made of potsherds are unsurpassed. Especially noteworthy is that the decorations are clearly influenced by the Southeast Asian style.

大厝的正脊和燕尾脊布满剪粘的装饰，突显出闽南传统民居独有的建筑风格

The central ridge and the swallow-tail ridge are covered with decorations that show the distinctive Southern Fujian style

房前屋内，不仅承载历史的记忆，更是主人寄托精神之所 / Exterior and interior views of the house

规尖的灰塑也是古厝的一道独特的风景 / The plaster sculpture shown here is also unique

灰塑做工精细，色彩艳丽 / Colorful plaster sculpture

门面的装饰，窗台的雕刻，处处展示出工艺魅力 / Decorations on the door and carvings on the windowsill

石雕工艺的巧妙运用，淋漓尽致

Folk tales and auspicious objects are
adopted for the building decorations

佳木门窗，装饰以各种金箔贴面的雕刻图案，展示主人富贵的心态

房梁上的额枋、雀替、斗拱、垂花柱显得堂皇恢弘／Inscribed tablets on the ridges, brackets, and wood carvings

屋内雕梁画栋，采光明暗相谐，虽陈旧却不失古典，似繁杂又不失规矩，可见匠人技艺的缜密与精湛

Decorations on the girders and pillars

围绕着房屋四周的彩绘、彩陶，构成了一道独特的风景线 / Decorations on the cornices

林厝（龙海）

位于龙海市东山村。建筑格局与普通闽南大厝有所不同，三幢均开侧门，既互相连通又各自独立。四边围建一圈房屋，均面向内院，二层高凸，像两座方形碉堡，类似闽西南土楼，室内装饰则保留闽南建筑风格。

The Lin Houses (Longhai)

Located in Dongshan village, Longhai, this large complex differs in style from other large southern Fujian homes. Each of the three large houses has its entrance on the side. Thus, although they are connected, each is also independent of the others. Each house is square with rooms on all four sides facing the inner courtyard. The second story is especially high, and looks like two square blockhouses. The construction style resembles that of the southwestern Fujian earthen buildings, but the interior decorations remain in the southern FuJian style.

古宅虽已苍老陈旧，但却是后人记忆中的故乡／ Historic residence

造型独特的垂花柱 / Carved "hanging flower" pillar

灰塑工艺是闽南建筑独有的装饰艺术 / Plaster sculptures are used only in Southern Fujian construction

大门、窗户，精雕细镂之间，大厝便有了自己的特色

This large mansion has its own character shown through its decorative carvings

林氏义庄（龙海）

位于龙海市角美镇浦尾村，清嘉庆二十四年（1819年）由台湾首富板桥林家第一代林平侯起建，两年后落成。南北长114米，东西宽90米。屋前有大池塘，石埕院，大厝主门侧开，红砖红瓦，燕尾脊，主屋与护厝纵横排列，沉稳大方。属典型的闽南建筑风格。林氏义庄是林氏家族内部的慈善建筑，于1821年开始运作，周济宗亲，1937年后被迫中断，持续了百余年。

The Lin Clan's Charity Mansion (Longhai)

This is located in Puwei village, Jiaomei town, Longhai. Construction on it began in 1819 with Lin Pinghou, of the first generation of the Lin family, and it was finished two years later. Lin was the richest man in Taiwan at the time. It is 114 meters long from north to south, 90 meters wide from east to west, and covers 3730 square meters of land. In front of the house are a large pond and a stone threshing ground. The main entrance opens at the side. Built of red bricks and red tiles, it has a swallow's tail roof. The building consists of main rooms and side rooms. It is well laid out and tasteful, typical of the southern Fujian style. The Lin clan's Charity Mansion was a mechanism for distributing charity to the clan. It began offering charitable relief to its members in 1821, and continued doing so for more than 100 years until it was forced to interrupt this activity by the anti-Japanese war in 1937.

厅堂 / A hall

通往大厝的小门 / A small connecting door

正厅两侧建筑对称布局，红砖青石铺地，严整有序而层次分明 / The two sides of the main hall are symmetrical

庄宅（晋江）

坐落在晋江市青阳大井口三角内15号，是一座五开间三落大厝，砖木结构，抬梁式和穿斗式混合架构，并附有回向、石埕和水井。大厝保存完好的木雕、石雕、砖雕制作精美，工艺精湛，是闽南古民居少有的"三雕"典范。

The Zhuang House (Jinjiang)

The Zhuang house—No. 15, Sanjiaonei, Qingyang—is a large home with five rooms situated transversely, and three sections in front and back. Built of brick and wood, it also has a stone threshing ground and a well. The home's perfectly preserved wood, stone, and brick carvings were skillfully executed. They are exquisite, and are a rare example of an historic house in southern Fujian having all three types of carving.

白石青石的巧妙运用，相得益彰／A building constructed of white and blue stone

院内回廊相接，天井阳光绿叶，温馨和谐／A courtyard with a winding corridor

庄宅大厝／A large country residence

古宅镂空石雕，技艺精湛，精美绝伦／An old residence with stone carvings and colored drawings

十八般武艺粉墨登场 / Carvings

垂花柱雕刻精细 / Carving

鸟语花香，吉祥如意 / A beautiful spring day

人物图案栩栩如生 / Lifelike images

房梁上的木构架是木雕装饰的重点，虽高高在上，但雕工却一丝不苟，件件都属上乘之作

The wood carvings on the girders are all masterpieces

房门、隔扇都是精致的木雕装饰，线条流畅，纹理细腻／Wood carvings on the archway and dividing screens

中宪第（南安）

　　位于南安市石井镇石井村，又称"九十九间"。清雍正年间，南安商人郑运锦从事对台贸易发家致富后，用巨款捐官"中宪大夫"，于1728年建成这座大型府第。建筑占地7780平方米，硬山顶，穿斗式木构架，砖石结构，宏伟壮丽。据说，实际上共有112间房屋，因非皇亲国戚，佯称99间。

Zhongxiandi (Nan'an)

　　Located in Shijing village, Shijing town, Nan'an, this house is also called "99 Rooms." During the period of the Yongzheng emperor [reigned 1723-1735] in the Qing dynasty, the Nan'an merchant Zheng Yunjin grew rich from trade with Taiwan, and donated a huge sum of money to purchase the official title of "Zhongxian Dafu." He built this large mansion in 1728. The structure occupies 7780 square meters of land. With a brick and stone framework, it is grand and spectacular. It's said that it actually has 112 rooms, but because Zheng Yunjin's social status did not allow him to have so many rooms, it was publicly claimed that it had only 99 rooms.

红砖、青石，灰塑工艺，见证着古厝的百年沧桑／Red bricks, blue stone, and plaster sculpturess

杨家大厝（石狮）

位于石狮市永宁镇后杆柄村，俗称"后杆柄九十九间古大厝"。由两部分组成，其前半部是始建于清代的传统民居杨家祖厝，后半部南洋风格的"六也楼"为旅菲华侨杨邦梭于1920年创建。整座大厝规模宏大，建筑面积约2万平方米，前后两部分建筑风格迥然不同，中西交融，互相衬托。

The Yang Family's Multi-storied Home (Shishi)

Located in Houganbing village, Yongning town, Shishi city, this is called "Houganbing's large historic 99-room house." It is made up of two parts. The front half of it is the Yang family's traditional ancestral home, which was built during the Qing dynasty; the back half is a building in the Southeast Asian style called "Liuye," which was built in 1920 by an overseas Chinese in the Philippines, Yang Bangsuo. The magnificent building sits on about 20,000 square meters of land. Although the styles of the front and back sections are very different, the Chinese and western parts blend well and complement each other.

三间两落、纵横交错的古厝群

Historic homes

瓦当、灰塑、檐口处的排水口，堂皇恢弘

Inscribed tablets on the ridges, brackets, and carved "hanging flower" pillar

The Historic Cai Family Home (Nan'an)

Situated in Zhang li village, Guanqiao town, Nan'an city, this home was built by an overseas Chinese in the Philippines, Cai Qichang, and his son Cai Zishen during the period from 1862 to 1911. The complex occupies more than 30,000 square meters of land, and includes sixteen quite well-preserved houses in five rows. It is a magnificent scene. Each building was constructed of white stone and red bricks with a curved roofline. All of the buildings have five rooms situated transversely, and two or three sections in the front and back. Although the buildings have these points in common, there are also certain individual differences. They retain the traditional southern Fujian style and also draw on some features of Southeast Asian architecture. At the same time, the historic Cai houses are also famous for their exquisite stone carving, brick carving, clay sculpture, and colorful drawings. They are called the grand museum of southern Fujian architecture.

蔡氏古民居（南安）

位于南安市官桥镇漳里村，由菲律宾华侨蔡启昌及其子蔡资深于清同治年间（1862年）至宣统三年（1911年）兴建。整个建筑群占地面积3万多平方米，共有较完整的宅第16座，分五行排列，场面宏大。其单体建筑，均为白石红砖建成，曲线屋脊，三进或二进五开间，但又有一定的个性差异。既保持了闽南传统风格，又吸收了南洋建筑的一些因素。蔡氏古民居还以精美的石雕、砖雕、泥塑、彩绘著称，被誉为闽南建筑大观园。

连排有序 / A perfect arrangement

前后整齐 / Everything in order

规模宏大 / On a magnificent scale

世裕厝 / Shiyu residence

彩楼厝 / Cailou residence

蔡浅厝 / Caiqian residence

德梯厝 / Deti residence

德典厝 / Dedian residence

世用厝 / Shiyong residence

攸楫厝 / Youji residence

世佑厝 / Shiyou residence

醉经堂 / Zuijing hall

中门护厝塌寿、走廊、房梁斗拱上的石雕、木雕、灰塑等技艺，相映成趣，对联、诗牌相得益彰，无处不显露出主人与艺人的独到匠心

Stone and wood carvings, plaster sculptures

祖宗灵牌、过道回廊，处处精雕细刻 / Ancestral tablets and winding corridor

大宅内的木雕工艺，达到闽南地区最高水平。花鸟鱼虫，人物故事，一刀一笔，惟妙惟肖，皆功到实处

The wood carving in the interior is the best in Southern Fujian

古色古香的盆架、座钟、瓦当、门当等都属古董中的精品 / Exquisite antiques: a frame for holding a flower basin, a xuanzhong, a tablet, and a mendang

垂花柱、供桌、眠床精雕细刻，溢彩鎏金 / "Hanging flower" pillar, altar table, and bed

塌寿的看墙上，石雕令人回味无穷，安详与恬然 / Stone carving

言简意赅、内涵丰富的石雕题词／An epigraph carved in stone

古厝的石雕堪称一绝，系名扬中外的惠安石雕师傅的工艺杰作／Stone carving from the famous Hui'an stone carving tradition

浮雕、透雕、影雕轮番上场，传统戏曲跃然墙上，散发出浓烈的生活气息，仿佛走进了一座艺术博物馆／Various kinds of stone carvings

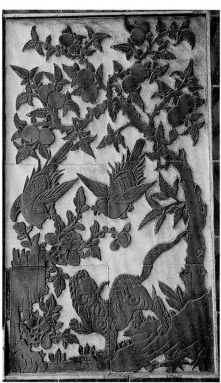

瓶、荷、狮、象、花鸟、神仙等装饰，散发出浓郁的生活气息 / Pottery objects on a wall—bottles, lotuses, lions, elephants, supernatural beings

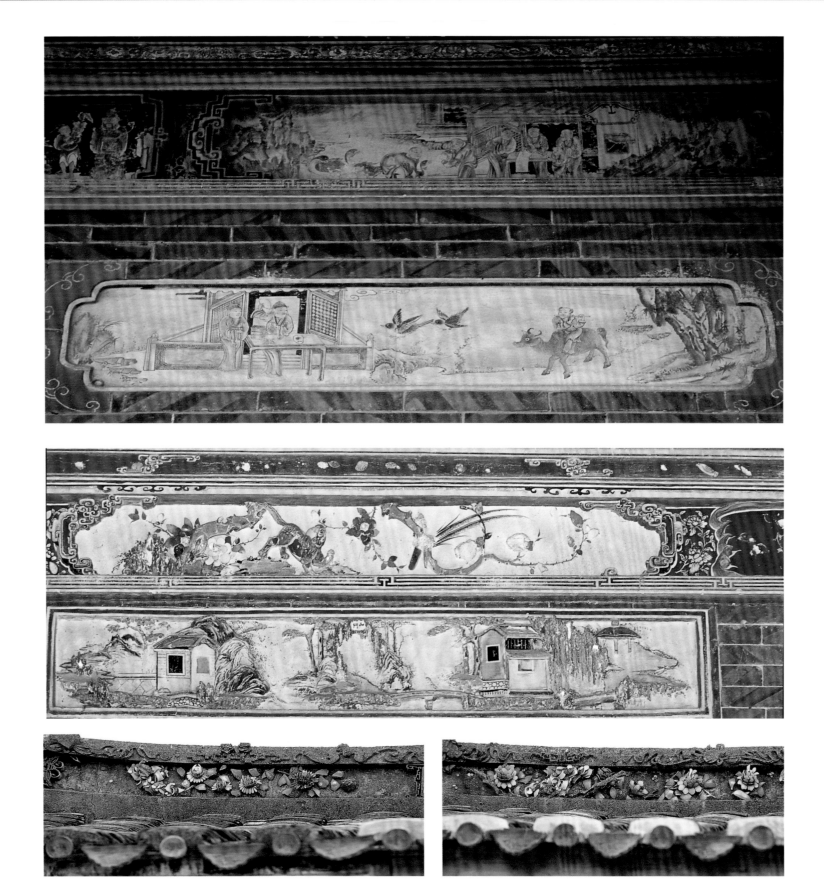

埕头间水车堵剪粘、彩绘，历经百年，如今还是色彩斑斓，清晰如初 / Color painting on the shuichedu

影雕，柔和细腻，犹如黑白摄影照片

Yingdiao—like a black and white photograph

大厝一字排开 / Front of the residence

鸳鸯大厝（仙游）

　　位于仙游县赖店镇坂头村。1927年，是在南洋经商的杨氏兄弟所建。房屋建筑形式属闽南模式，屋内木雕、石雕、灰雕工艺精湛，两幢房屋建筑规格大小一样，一字排开，既统一又是各自独立。

The Yuanyang residence(Xianyou)

　　Located in Bantou village, Laidian town, Xianyou city.　Built in 1927 in the Southern Fujian style.　The interior has wood and stone carvings, as well as plaster sculptures.　The two buildings are the same size. ▬▬▬▬▬▬▬

大厝从里到外，透露出名士遗风，历史的荣耀之光若隐若现 ／ Plaster sculptures, white stone, and ridge carving with gold-leaf

各种雕饰艺术融为一体，乡土气息浓郁 / All kinds of carvings are blended together here

塌寿看墙的砖雕工艺 / Plaster sculptures

跨进大门，门窗木雕彩画随处可见／Wood carvings and colored drawings are everywhere

仙水大厅（仙游）

位于仙游县榜头镇仙水村，建于明正统十一年（1446年），总面积8820平方米，坐北朝南，依山势建成四座并排的"九间厢"大厝，门前还有一口面积4000平方米的弧形风水池。

Xianshui hall (Xianyou) ▄▄▄▄▄▄

The large, south-facing Xianshui hall, located in Xianshui village, Bangtou town, Xianyou county, was constructed in 1446. It is 8820 square meters in area. In front of it is a pond that is 4000 square meters.

雕刻精湛的石鼓，不失当年的风采 / A carved stone drum

厢房走廊宽大、明亮 / Corridor

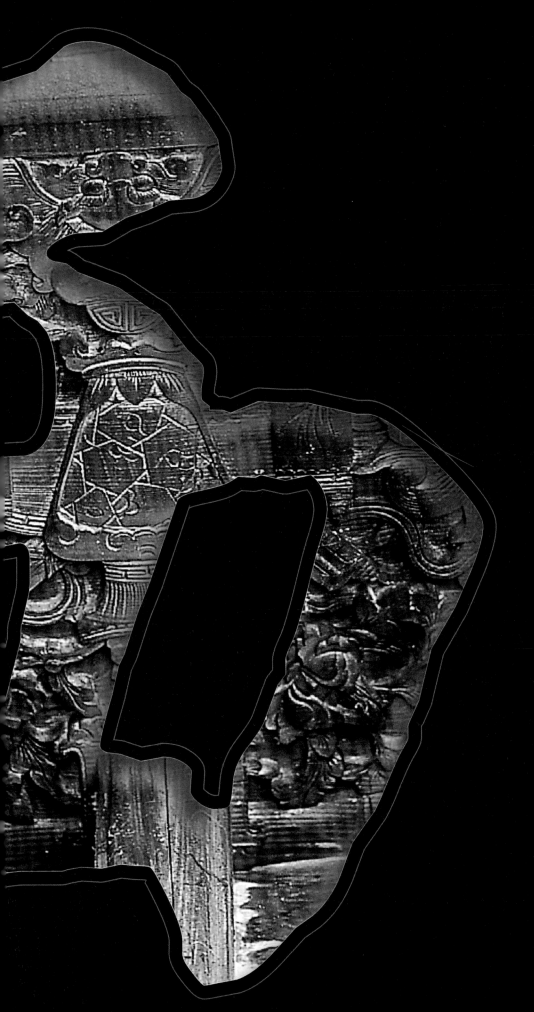

闽南古民居

闽西一般指古汀州府辖境客家人居住地区。客家民系入闽较迟，其语言和风俗，与福建其他民系有较大的差异。

由于长途辗转迁徙，客家人具有特别强烈的宗族意识和正统观念。《礼记》说："君子将营宫室，宗庙为先。"这话为客家人所尊崇。在闽西许多村落，最豪华的建筑是家族宗祠。气势非凡的上杭李氏大宗祠，堪称客家宗祠的代表。

闽西是山区，经济比较落后，古民居以土木结构为主。其南片永定、武平、上杭地区多土楼，北片长汀、宁化、连城等地多为府第式古民居，通常是多进合院，与其他地区差异不大。长汀、连城一带有一种被称为"九厅十八井"的大型民居，中央为多进厅堂，两旁各有一排或两排横屋，院落重重，房间众多，反映了客家人聚族而居四世同堂的生活方式。天井和晒坪用鹅卵石精心铺地，较有特色。

闽西保存完好的客家古村落，当属连城县的培田村和芷溪村。

Traditional Houses in Western Fujian

Western Fujian, the region where the Hakka people live, is the area administered in the past by Tingzhou prefecture. The Hakka people entered Fujian relatively late; their language and customs are quite different from those of other peoples in Fujian.

Because of their migration over long distances, the Hakka people have a very strong clan consciousness and respect for Confucian orthodoxy. The Book of Rites says: "When gentlemen build their homes, the ancestral temple takes priority." These words can be taken as a depiction of the Hakka. In many western Fujian villages, the most elaborate buildings are the clan ancestral temples. The unusual, grand Li ancestral temple in Shanghang is representative of the Hakka ancestral temples.

Western Fujian is a mountainous region, and the economy is relatively undeveloped. Earth and wood are the main construction materials used for the traditional homes. In the southern part of this region - Yongding, Wuping, and Shanghang - most of the houses are earthen buildings. In the northern part - Changting, Ninghua, and Liancheng - the traditional homes are in the style of mansions. As a rule, there are multiple sections and courtyards; in this, they are not much different from other regions. The Changting-Liancheng region has a kind of large-scale home that is called "nine halls and eighteen courtyards." Along the central axis are the main sections of rooms and courtyards. Each of the two sides has one or two rows of side rooms, many courtyards, and numerous rooms, thus reflecting the Hakka people's lifestyle of four generations living together. The courtyards and threshing grounds laid with cobblestones are quite distinctive.

The well-preserved old Hakka villages are Peitian hamlet and Zhixi hamlet in Liancheng county.

培田古民居（连城）

　　培田古村落位于连城县宣和乡，全村300余户全部姓吴。相传吴姓先祖早在1344年便迁居培田，繁衍至今已历30世。

　　它由30幢高堂华屋，21座吴氏宗祠，6处书院，2座跨街牌坊，以及4条千米长街组成。民居群紧密有序、错落有致，外墙全部为青色防火砖，内为木制构架，门楼泥塑石雕，屋脊飞檐彩陶，窗、梁、屏上都有木刻雕花彩绘漆画，做工精细，用料考究，工艺精湛。古建筑多为"九厅十八井"式，典型的客家建筑模式。

The Historic Houses in Peitian (Liancheng)

　　The old Peitian hamlet is in Xuanhe village, Liancheng county. The more than 300 families there are all surnamed Wu. It is said that the earliest Wu ancestor moved to Peitian in 1344, and the clan has flourished in the thirty generations since then.

　　The village's four 1000-meter-long streets are made up of thirty big houses, twenty-one ancestral temples for the Wu clan, six academies, and two archways spanning the streets. The traditional homes are built close together, but with a pleasing sense of order. The entire outer wall is made of fireproof blue tiles. Inside it, the buildings are wooden. On the arches are clay sculptures and stone carvings. The roofs and upturned eaves are decorated with ancient painted pottery. The windows, girders, and screens are festooned with wood carvings and lacquer paintings. The materials were selected with care and the craftsmanship is exquisite. Most of the old structures are in the "nine halls and eighteen courtyards" style; this is the quintessence of the Hakka architectural style.

山环水绕的培田村／ *Panoramic view of Peitian village*

屋瓦相连，门楼相望／Tiles and archways

平常人家，却总忍不住猜测其昔日的奢华

An ordinary home, but people can't help but imagine how luxurious it was in the past

充满诗情的街巷 / A street filled with a sense of poetry

岁月流逝，生活依旧 / The years have rolled on, but life is the same as always

透过花窗展现其文化内涵 / A decorated window

细节中的生动 / An attractive detail

农家院落／A farm family's courtyard

古老的家具／Old furniture

去年的门神 / Door gods from the past

雕花之美 / The beauty of carving

精美的垂花柱／A beautiful carved flower hanging from a pillar

芷溪古民居（连城）

　　连城县庙前镇芷溪村，是一个由6个自然村组成、万人居住的客家古村落。明清以来，先后兴建了68座古祠，138幢古民居。除部分为祭祖联宗之用外，大多数是祠居合一的复合型建筑，普遍采用客家地区的"九厅十八井"结构布局，庭院舒畅，雕梁画栋，飞檐翘角，美轮美奂。客家人慎终追远，敬祖睦宗的传统美德在这里得到充分的体现。

The Historic Zhixi Houses (Liancheng)

　　Zhixi village in Miaoqian town, Liancheng county, is made up of six natural villages. It is an old village where 10,000 Hakka people live. Beginning in the Ming and Qing dynasties, sixty-eight ancestral temples and 138 traditional homes were built. Apart from some that are exclusively for ancestor worship, most are complexes that combine ancestral temples and homes. They generally adopted the Hakka region's "nine halls and eighteen courtyards" style. The courtyards are spacious. There are carved girders, painted ridgepoles, and eaves upturned at the corners. They are very beautiful. The traditional virtues of commemorating the ancestors and living in harmony with people of the same clan are fully realized here.

振翅欲飞的门楼 / An arch

祠居合一是芷溪
古民居的特色，每座
门楼都像祠庙

The distinctive feature of the historic buildings in Zhixi is that they combine ancestral temples and homes. The front of each house resembles an ancestral temple

庭院宽大，是祭祖等公共活动的场所 ／ The courtyard is wide and large; it is the space for worship of the ancestors and other public events

精美的雕刻艺术，炫耀着祖先显赫的地位

Fine carvings

李氏大宗祠（上杭）

　　位于上杭县稔田镇官田村，为纪念李氏始祖李火德而建，俗称"火德公祠"。

　　李氏大宗祠占地5600平方米，规模宏大，气势不凡。宗祠系三进四直的砖木结构建筑，有3个大厅和26间中小客厅，住房104间。宗祠左右对称展开，结构严谨，秩序井然，充分体现了客家宗法礼制传统下的建筑追求，是福建客家宗祠的典型代表。

The Li Clan's Large Ancestral Hall (Shanghang)

Located in Guantian village , Rentian town , Shanghang county , it was built to commemorate the Li clan's earliest ancestor Li Huode, and is called the "Huode Ancestral Hall."

It occupies 5600 square meters of land. Magnificent and extraordinary, it has three sections and four straight intersecting aisles built of tiles and wood. It has three large halls and twenty-six reception rooms of various sizes. There are 104 other rooms. The left and right sides are symmetrical; it is a very precise structure. It embodies the traditional architectural aims of the Hakka people's patriarchal clan system. It is the quintessential representative of the ancestral halls of the Fujian Hakka people.

中轴线对称展开的李氏大宗祠，造型优美 / The Li clan's ancestral hall.A beautifully designed symmetrical building

闽北地区位于闽江上游，是北方汉族移民最早进入福建并开发的地区，包括古代建宁、延平、邵武三府辖境，也就是今天南平市的全境和三明市的部分县市。

闽北文化在宋代高度发达，科举和学术人才众多。朱熹在闽北讲学数十年，建立了著名的理学学派闽学。从元代开始，朱子学说成了历朝官方意识形态的理论基础，影响深远。

闽北是山区，盛产杉木，传统民居以土木和砖木结构为主。平面布局多以天井为中心的多进合院式，杉木构架，外墙以夯土或砌砖围护。豪宅多为"三厅九栋"的青砖灰瓦建筑。闽北古民居受徽派建筑影响，风火墙高大硬朗，形成错落的梯级形态；其装饰以砖雕最为精彩，多体现在门楼；木雕工艺也相当出色。

现存古民居，广泛分布于各县乡镇村落，多建于清代。泰宁县的尚书第建于明天启年间，保存完好，为最早和最重要的一座。邵武的和平古镇、金坑乡，武夷山市的下梅村、城村都保存着成片的传统民居。浦城、建阳、建瓯、政和、尤溪等地，也有不少遗存。

闽北传统民居青砖黛瓦，质朴深沉而又风骨凛然，体现了理学文化的丰厚积淀，具有很高的审美价值。

Traditional Houses in Northern Fujian

Northern Fujian is located on the upper reaches of the Min River. The earliest region entered and developed by the northern Han people, it comprises the three historical administrative prefectures of Jianning, Yanping, and Shaowu (today's Nanping and part of the county seat of Sanming).

Northern Fujian culture developed to a high degree during the Song dynasty. Throngs of scholars took the imperial examinations and were engaged in learning. Zhu Xi gave lectures in northern Fujian for decades and established a branch of Neo-Confucianism: Min learning. Zhu Xi's doctrine of Neo-Confucianism remained central to China as its state orthodoxy from the late Song dynasty until the early 20th Century; it had far-reaching influence.

Northern Fujian is a mountainous area with a lot of large firs. Traditional houses were built mostly of earth and wood or of bricks and wood. The courtyard served as the center of the house. The supporting framework was made of fir. The outer wall was built of rammed earth or bricks and tiles. Most of the luxurious homes were built of blue bricks and gray tiles and included "three rows of rooms with a large hall in the middle." People in northern Fujian were influenced by Anhui-style architecture, which included a large, high firewall. Its contour had a random, step-like cadence. The most splendid parts of the ornamentation were the brick carvings, most of which were on the arches. The wood carving was also quite fine.

Most of the extant historic houses located in each county, village, and town were built during the Qing dynasty. Shangshudi in Taining county was built during the early Ming dynasty, and has been perfectly preserved. It is the earliest and most important of the buildings. Quite a lot of other traditional houses have been preserved in the ancient town of Heping and Jinkeng village in Shaowu, and Xiamei village in Wuyishan city. Others are preserved in Pucheng, Jianyang, Jian'ou, Zhenghe, and Youxi.

The blue bricks and black tiles of northern Fujian's traditional homes, the rusticity and the stern vigor, embody the rich Neo-Confucian culture and are very tasteful.

村口／Entrance to the village

城村全景／A panoramic view of Chengcun

城村民居（武夷山）

城村坐落在武夷山市闽越王城遗址附近。城村是古代闽越人离去后，中原移民重建的村庄，因建在西汉闽越国城邑的土地上，故名"古粤（越）城村"。

该村历史悠久，古朴幽静，至今仍保留着明清传统建筑的大体风貌。木牌坊，宗祠，青砖大瓦房，街巷，古井，牌匾，记载着这座古村落发展的历史。尤为精彩的是古民居细部的各种砖雕石刻。

Chengcun Houses (WuyiShan)

Cheng village lies in the vicinity of the site of the Minyue king's capital in Wuyishan city. Cheng village was rebuilt by migrants from the central plains after the ancient autochthonous Minyue people left. Because it was built in the Minyue kingdom's capital of the western Han dynasty [206 B.C.-9 A.D.], it is called "the historic Yue Chengcun."

Very old, Chengcun is simple, unsophisticated, and solitary. In general, it preserved the traditional Ming-Qing style. There are: a wooden archway; an ancestral hall; a large blue brick house with a tiled roof; streets and alleys; an old well; and tablets recording the historical development of this village. The most splendid features lie in the carved brick and inscribed stone under the pillars, on the eaves, above the windows, and so forth.

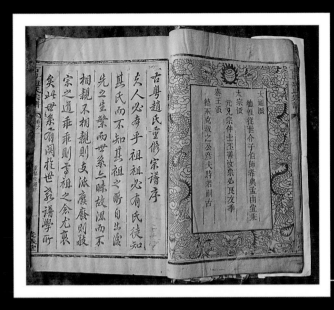

根据族谱，村里的赵姓是宋皇室的后裔

According to the genealogical records, the Zhao family was a descendant of the Song dynasty's imperial family

赵氏家祠内景 / The interior of the Zhao family ancestral temple

百岁坊，纪念赵氏家族一位高寿的祖先

100-year lane: commemorating a long-lived ancestor of the Zhao family

精美的石雕 / Exquisite brick carvings and stone inscriptions

林氏家祠门墙上的砖雕装饰，非常漂亮

The Lin family ancestral temple. The front wall has very beautiful brick carvings

充满沧桑的细节 / Traces of the past

下梅古民居（武夷山）

　　位于武夷山市区东南12公里的下梅村。清朝初年，下梅村是武夷山的重要茶叶集散地，空前繁荣。鸦片战争后，渐渐衰败下来。

　　下梅村是闽北保存最好的古村落之一，基本上维持着清代的建筑格局。数十座明清风格的古民居分列于长达900余米的当溪两旁。豪宅大屋，街路古井，小桥流水，体现了南方水乡建筑的特色。村中随处可见各种雕花门楼，工艺精湛，堪称闽北民居砖雕艺术的代表。

The Old Xiamei Houses (WuyiShan)

They are located in Xiamei village 12 kilometers southeast of Wuyishan city. In the early Qing dynasty, Xiamei village was an important distribution center for tea from WuyiShan, and enjoyed unprecedented prosperity. After the Opium War [1839-42], it declined in importance.

Xiamei village, one of the best-preserved villages in northern Fujian, essentially maintains the architectural style of the Qing dynasty. Dozens of Ming-Qing-style homes stand on both sides of the more than 900-meter-long brook. These large, imposing homes on streets with ancient wells and small bridges are the quintessence of buildings in the southern water villages. You can see all kinds of decorative carved arches everywhere in the village. The superb craftsmanship is typical of the brick carving in northern Fujian homes.

溪旁的"美人靠"，依旧发挥其实用功能 / Parapet at the side of a brook

邹氏家祠，闽北最精彩的雕花门楼之一 ／ The Zou family ancestral temple.One of the best examples of decorative carved arches in northern Fujian

芭蕉扇门 / Bottle-shaped door

邹氏家祠后院 / The back courtyard of the Zou family ancestral temple

散落在古宅中的石雕随处可见 / Stone carving

形态各异的砖雕 / Various brick carvings

邹氏家祠门楼局部 / Part of the arch of the Zou family ancestral temple

彩绘艺术不失艳丽 / Colored drawings

木雕内容丰富多彩 / Wood carvings

和平古镇（邵武）

　　位于邵武市西南部的和平镇，系福建保存完好的大型城堡式村镇之一。外有城墙谯楼，内有纵横交织的古街巷，以及上百座明清古民居。自五代黄峭创办"和平书院"以来，宗族办学成风，历代教育发达，科举兴盛，人才辈出。现存古建筑有义仓、宫庙、宗祠、府第等，仅"大夫第"就有三幢。

Ancient Heping Town (Shaowu)

　　Heping town in the southwestern part of Shaowu is one of the best preserved large-scale fortress-style towns. Surrounding the town are the rampart and watchtowers; inside, the town is crisscrossed with old streets and alleys, as well as more than 100 homes from Ming and Qing times. From the time ground was broken in the Five Dynasties era for the "Heping Academy," the clans established schools that flourished. Education developed over the ages: men achieved success in the imperial examinations, and scholars emerged in large numbers. The extant historic buildings include a charity granary, temples, ancestral halls, and mansions, including three called "Dafudi" [high official's residence].

书院、门楼至今依然完好，古色古香 / Archway

古床、门窗不仅有实用功能，还具有"养眼"效果 / Old bed, doors, and windows

精美的木雕细节，显示出工匠的高超技艺／Wood carving—close-up view

金坑古民居（邵武）

金坑古民居群位于邵武市西45公里的金坑乡，四五十座，连片建筑，因保存不善，毁损比较严重。其中"儒林郎"、"九级厅"为精品，前者的砖雕和木雕非常出色。街巷多铺鹅卵石，别有风韵。金坑的古宅，屋墙夯土或砌砖，高大结实，窗户却特别窄小。大约因为是山区，从前匪患严重，建房特别注重防御功能。

The Old Jinkeng Houses (Shaowu)

The group of historic Jinkeng houses is located in Jinkeng village, 45 kilometers west of Shaowu county. There are about forty or fifty houses adjacent to one another, but they have not been well-preserved. The best ones are "Rulinlang" and "Jiujiting." The stone and wood carving in the former are really fine. The streets and alleys are paved with cobblestones a particularly charming feature. In Jinkeng's old buildings, the walls are rammed earth or brick; they are high, large, and strong. The windows, however, are very narrow and small. Probably because this is a mountainous region and banditry was a serious problem in the past, when they built these houses, they paid particular attention to their utility for defense.

连片的金坑古民居 / Old houses in Jinkeng

鹅卵石小巷，饶有风韵 / A small alley paved with cobblestones

文昌阁 / The Wenchang pavilion

村内巷道空间格局完整，古风犹存；民居、祠堂形式多样，丰富多彩

Village street, residences, and ancestral temples

儒林郎木雕，刀法明快，构图简洁，意趣动人

Wood carving at Rulinlang: its skillful, concise composition is attractive

砖雕繁复，工艺精湛 / Brick carving

观前古村（浦城）

位于浦城县东南23公里的南浦溪畔，村口有一所道观，故称观前。从前为重要的水运码头，非常繁华。现存不少明清建筑，多筑土墙，依山就势，临溪一排吊脚楼。观前堪称一个用鹅卵石垒出来的村庄。街巷，台阶，护坡，沟渠，庭院，天井，都以鹅卵石密密铺砌，坚实优美，又别致动人。

The Old Village of Guanqian (Pucheng)

On the southern bank of the Pu River 23 kilometers southeast of Pucheng county, the village entrance has a Taoist temple, and so the village is called Guanqian [in front of the Taoist temple]. In the past, it was an important bustling cargo port. Quite a few Ming and Qing buildings are extant. Most of them have earthen walls and are built against the slope. A row of houses was built along the riverbank; the rear parts of these houses are over the water. One may say that Guanqian is a village made of cobblestones. The streets, steps, retaining walls on hills, ditches, and courtyards are all laid with them. They are stable, elegant, and spectacularly charming.

祠堂 / Ancestral temple

鹅卵石铺成的图案 / The charm of cobblestones

鹅卵石垒出来的村庄 / The village made of cobblestenes

休闲、聊天的场所 / A place to rest and chat

沿溪而建的"美人靠" / Parapet on the riverside

土墙黛瓦，沿溪而立 / Earthen wall and black tiles, standing along the stream

杨源民居（政和）

　　政和县杨源村，最具有特色的是穿过村心的九曲鲤鱼溪，据说是按风水学原理故意凿出的。乡规民约，禁止捕捞溪里的鲤鱼。杨源村人多半姓张，为唐末武将张谨的后裔，村落至今还保持清代的格局。民居是一色的土墙黛瓦，分列鲤鱼溪两旁，十分优美。山墙为平直的马头墙，依然是典型的闽北建筑风格。

鲤鱼溪 / Carp Stream

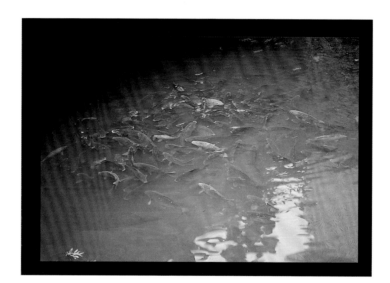

The Yangyuan House (Zhenghe)

The most distinctive feature of Yangyuan village in Zhenghe county is the Nine-Bend Carp Stream that runs through the center of the village. It is said that it was deliberately dug out to conform to the principles of fengshui. The villagers came to an agreement prohibiting catching the river carp. Most of the people in the village are named Zhang: they are the descendants of the late-Tang dynasty general Zhang Jin. The village preserves its Qing dynasty style. The elegant houses, all with earthen walls and black tiles, stand along both sides of the Carp Stream. The contours of the front wall are step-like, with straight lines: this is typical of northern Fujian construction.

村尾廊桥 / A covered bridge at the end of the village

街巷小景 / Street scene

闽北古民居 — 杨源民居
TRADITIONAL HOUSES IN NORTHERN FUJIAN ▊ THE YANGYUAN HOUSE

尚书第（泰宁）

　　尚书第位于泰宁县城，为明代兵部尚书李春烨的府第，建于明天启末年（1627年前后），至今已有380多年的历史。尚书第有主宅5幢、辅房8栋，分5道门沿甬道一字排列，除厅堂、天井、回廊外，有房120余间，全为砖石木结构。每幢主宅均为三进。整个府第宏伟壮观，布局严谨，具有高超的建筑水平。

　　尚书第与紧邻的明代早期建筑世德堂，以及李氏宗祠，共同构成尚书第建筑群，包含古代官居、民宅、祠堂、客厅、辅房、大庭院等多种功能建筑，是福建现存规模最大、保存最完整的明代民居建筑群，列为第三批全国重点文物保护单位。

Shangshudi (Taining)

　　Shangshudi is located in Taining's county seat. It was the official residence of a Ming dynasty defense minister, Li Chunye. Built during the late Ming (about 1627), it is now more than 380 years old. It has five main buildings and eight subsidiary buildings facing the same main corridor. In addition to the halls, the courtyards, and the corridors, there are more than 120 other rooms, all built of brick, stone, and wood. Each main building has three sections separated by courtyards. The residence is grand and spectacular, and precise in its overall layout.

　　Shangshudi and its neighbors, the Shide hall built in the early Ming dynasty and the Li family ancestral hall, constitute the group of Shangshudi buildings. These include the historic official residences, people's homes, ancestral halls, reception rooms, other rooms, and large courtyards. It is the largest extant complex of buildings, and these are the most perfectly preserved traditional homes from the Ming dynasty. This complex is also on the third list of key cultural relics under state protection.

气势宏伟的尚书第，青砖灰瓦，质朴大方。高大的马头墙错落起伏，风骨硬朗
The vigorous, grand Shangshudi: with blue bricks and gray tiles, it is modest and tasteful. The contours of the large, high wall undulate

深邃的青石甬道 ／ The path paved with blue stone

庭院深深 / The courtyard

石碑 / Stone tablet

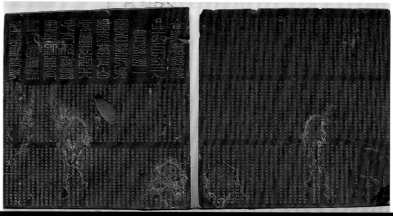

豪门沧桑 / The main door

浑厚大气的石雕 / Stone carving

严整华美的木雕 / Wood carving